Feed me!

The fresh daisy Cookbook for Babies and Toddlers

Gerrie Hawes with Bruce Hudson and Ali Hanan

Kyle Cathie Ltd

*For giggling Sandra, time for tennis Malcolm
and in loving memory of my grandparents,
Daisy and Percy, Elsie and Walter.*

This book contains general advice and recipes suitable for babies
and children. If you have specific concerns, special dietary needs or
a family history of allergies or food intolerances you should seek the
advice of your health visitor or other specialist medical practitioner.

First published in Great Britain in 2005 by
Kyle Cathie Limited
122 Arlington Road, London NW1 7HP
general.enquiries@kyle-cathie.com
www.kylecathie.com

10 9 8 7 6 5 4 3 2 1

ISBN 1 85626 615 X

Senior editor: Muna Reyal
Designer: Alison Fenton
Photographer: Sandra Lane
Stylist: Cathy Sinker
Food stylists: Krissy Schmidt,
    Jacqueline Bellefontaine and Lizzie Harris
Copy editor: Anne Newman
Editorial assistant: Cecilia Desmond
Production: Sha Huxtable and Alice Holloway

A Cataloguing In Publication record for this title is available
from the British Library.

Colour reproduction by Sang Choy

Printed and bound in China by C & C Offset Printing Company Ltd

Feed me!

Contents

FOREWORD

Why *Feed me!*

Feed me! evolved from conversations I had with parents while working on Fresh Daisy. This is a book for real parents living in the real world. There is nothing complicated about making delicious babyfood – but there are some basics you need to know before you dive in.

I start with recipes for you, not only to encourage you to think about your own relationship with food before you start teaching your child, but also because there's now evidence that babies start to develop taste preferences before the first purée passes their lips.

Feed me! is also for parents who look through cookery books for babies and toddlers and say, 'How the hell do they expect me to decorate babyfood with eyes, ears and toenails when I've got a screaming child scattering toys around the room?' Hey, I hear you. Hopefully you'll find my approach a refreshing change.

Developing a good relationship with food

Learning to eat well and educate the palate is as important as learning your abc's, which is why I want to introduce your baby to the tastes and textures of *real* food. Studies by Dr Gillian Harris at Birmingham University show that the foods you feed your baby now will have a profound effect on their health for life. If you consider that nearly a quarter of all children in the UK are overweight by the age of 11 as well as the mounting evidence that behaviour and brain development are affected by diet, it does raise the question: if we are what we eat, then what on earth are our children eating? What could be better than the real taste, natural colour and wholesome nutrition of fresh fruit, vegetables, meat and fish?

Ultimately your baby should eat as you do. Besides, life's just too short to make everyone's favourite meals every night. That's one of the many reasons why we've included a section of deliciously healthy meals for you and why most of the toddler dishes are adaptable to adult tastes.

Why Fresh Daisy?

As somebody who is passionate about the taste, textures and flavours of food, working for a major food manufacturer was a surprisingly depressing eye opener. Every time I visited the factory, it didn't matter whether it was babyfood, tomato soup, pasta in sauce or baked beans being cooked, it always had the same underlying smell. It's an odd, not completely unpleasant smell, but very different from what you'd smell in a domestic kitchen. This was when the light bulb started to flash. I was working on toddler food, and began to question why children seem to have such a taste for highly processed food. I could only assume that taste preferences develop very early on, which drew my attention to the standard of commercially available babyfood.

I launched the Fresh Daisy range of babyfoods in 2003 – using the simple principles any parent would use if time permitted: the best organic seasonal food, sourced direct from the farmer whenever possible; steaming freshly prepared ingredients without the addition of anti-browning or other processing agents, then fast freezing in individual portions. Simple. Pure.

I began to realise that the reliance on overprocessed food was an extremely damaging way to bring up a child. My fears were confirmed when we started to do tastings at baby shows. Babies brought up on long-life jars, tins and pots wouldn't eat our product yet those brought up on home-made food lapped it up. Nursery owners also vented their frustration at having to 'rewean' babies off sterilised babyfood on to home-made food by gradually reintroducing fresh products.

I urge you to have a go at making at least one or two of the cooked purées yourself – and compare the taste, colour and texture to those of long-life babyfood. Once you've tasted frozen babyfood (your own or shop-bought) I think you'll find it hard to reach for the jar.

The future

Having tried to ignore my desire to revolutionise babyfood for eight years I was inspired by my now husband to have a go, influenced by that typical pioneering spirit New Zealanders seem to foster. Fresh Daisy feels more like a vocation than a business – success is seeing the quality of babyfood significantly improve and parents understanding that it really does matter what a baby eats.

So *vive la révolution*! Three years after launching I'm still battling away trying to convince the major supermarkets to change the whole babyfood sector. It's very much two steps forward and one step back or maybe a bit more the other way round. But what hasn't changed is my passion for improving the standard of commercially available babyfood.

Recipe for success?

Thanks for buying the book, enjoy the journey, experiment with tastes for you and your baby and help spread the word that fresh is best. And remember if you haven't got time to make your own, there's always a great alternative in the freezer of the babyfood aisle!

Gerie Hawes

Introduction

A beginner's guide on how and what to feed your baby. Everything from a nutritional guide to the right equipment to buy (and even a word about poo).

How to use this book

You come first

This book starts with you. Yes, your baby is important, but so are you. A happy parent usually means a happy baby, which is why I've started the recipes as soon as the baby is born because a well-balanced, healthy diet will improve your energy levels and general well-being at a period when sleep, time and patience are in extremely short supply. So I've kept it short and sweet. These recipes are easy to prepare and easily adapted. They are rich in vitamins, proteins, nutrients and all-round goodness to keep you functioning at your peak. I've also tried to introduce some interesting tastes and flavours which may have dropped off your radar. Parents will be interested to read that babies' taste preferences are influenced by what their mother eats during breastfeeding. A study in 2001 (Manella, Jagnow & Beauchamp) showed that the babies of mothers who drank carrot juice while breastfeeding consumed more carrot-flavoured baby rice. The more varied a mother's diet the more likely it is that the baby will take to different foods during weaning.

Sing while you're weaning

If you've hit the weaning stage you'll notice that all the recipes suggested are single variants of fruit or vegetables. I do this for a couple of reasons: first because giving them adult combinations like beef and vegetable risotto or cottage pie (as some commercial companies do) may be great after a session down the pub but for a baby who has had nothing but milk it's going to be a bit of a mind boggle. The second reason is because it's a good way to monitor if there are any allergies. I suggest introducing each variant earlier in the day, either mid-morning or at lunchtime for a couple of days, to get your child used to them and give you time to check for any reactions. Then you can move on to another fruit or veg.

Shaping recipes

Wherever possible, I've created the recipes as single servings so you can try a small amount on your child without having to make large batches, but all recipes can be increased in size proportionately depending on how many children you have, how hungry they are or whether you have a moment to do a job lot and some home freezing. The recipes are intended as a starting point – feel free to change the ingredients using inspirations from the stage you are at or from previous stages. Just because a food is in stage 2 doesn't mean your baby shouldn't enjoy it at stages 3, 4 and beyond. The stage 2s, like peach, plum and vanilla (brilliant with vanilla ice cream) and squash and red lentil (add a dash of pepper, maybe a little salt and then a swirl of sour cream for a delicious adult soup), could be in your diet forever more. Going the other way, however, is a definite no-no. A stage 2 meal must not be given to a stage 1 baby. I've also shown you ways to use less common fruit and veg so if your baby takes to them adapt later stage recipes to incorporate them. Most of the recipes can be made into adult versions with a slight adaptation (or just a bit of seasoning) so you won't have to spend hours in the kitchen cooking for your children and then again for yourself.

Commercial babyfoods

In a perfect world every parent would cook every meal from fresh organic produce. It would also put my company Fresh Daisy out of business. The reality is, even the busiest parent has days when time runs away from them and cooking meals from scratch is impossible.

Commercially available babyfood fills the gap for days like these. Up until recently jars and tins have dominated the market. These are convenient because they can sit in the cupboard for two to three years and be pulled out in times of crisis. The problem for a parent who does most of their own cooking is that their child won't be familiar with the taste of this kind of food. Imagine cooking a piece of broccoli to 121°C (250°F) in a pressure cooker and you'll begin to understand why food from tins and

jars loses its colour and texture and also tastes considerably different from home-made food.

Recently there has been a move towards yogurt-style pots. This is in reaction to the discovery of a potential cancer-causing carcinogen (semicarbazide) leaching from the jar's lid seal into the food. Despite the different format, the food is still sterilised and tastes the same as the jars and tins.

Frozen babyfoods

If you are looking for a product that replicates home cooking then frozen babyfood, cooked from fresh (rather than concentrate), organic ingredients, is the best option. Freezing enables gentler cooking without destroying taste, colour and texture. You'll find it much easier to swap from good-quality frozen babyfoods to home-made food as they will taste the same.

LEFT: **Carrot purée**, see page 60

Read the label

It's a good idea to get used to reading and understanding food labels to appreciate exactly what you are putting into your baby's mouth because organic doesn't automatically mean healthy. Watch out for really sweet cereals, which may shout organic goodness from the packet, but if you read the ingredients you'll see huge amounts of sugar.

Cereal or breakfast bars are among the worst offenders. They may look nutritious, but contain more than three times the amount of sugar recommended by the Food Standards Agency.

What to look out for

Much of it is learning to interpret food jargon and which additives to stay away from. The ingredients are listed in order of quantity – so if a product lists sugar as the first ingredient, then it's full of sugar. Food manufacturers will often try to mask sugar content by citing its many different states so look out for sucrose, maltose, dextrose, fructose, maltodextrose, glucose, lactose, cane sugar, mannotose, corn syrup, inverted sugar, sugar syrup and the rather cunningly worded hydrolised starch.

Then there's the artificial sweeteners, including Aspartame, Acesulfame K and Sodium Saccharine. These are all banned in foods for children under the age of 3 years, so you won't find them lurking in a jar of babyfood but they are still present in all sorts of unlikely savoury snacks and soft drinks, including squash.

Other rather unappetising monikers are 'mechanically recovered', or 'separated meat'. This literally means meat leftovers because it is made from the remains of the carcass of an animal once all the good meat has gone…mmmmmm nice!

E numbers and additives

The e in E numbers stands for Europe and was developed to regulate what is and isn't permitted as an additive in food. Every additive in food has an E number which you may find on the label. Recently manufacturers have been using the scientific name for additives as there has been a backlash against E numbers.

So what are the main culprits to look out for? Well, there is a whole line-up. Take tartrazine as an example: the yellow food colouring, E102, is currently behind bars for being linked to allergic reactions, asthma, growth retardation and hyperactivity in kids.

But just to confuse the issue, some E numbers are completely natural and harmless. The following is a quick guide to E numbers to look out for. As a rule, babies and children can react badly to azo dye colours and benzoate preservatives.

The following E numbers should not be given to babies and young children:
Preservatives E213, E214, E215, E216, E217, E218, E219.
Antioxidants E310, E311, E312.
Sweeteners E420, E421, E951 (aspartame) has been at the centre of several health scares, E954 (saccharine) is linked to cancer and tumours in animals.
Flavourings E621 (monosodium glutamate), E622, E623, E627, E631, E635.
Others to avoid E407, E513, E524, E525 and E541.

E numbers to avoid for children:
Food colourings E102, E104, E107, E110, E120, E122, E123, E124, E127, E128, E132, E133, E150, E151, E154, E155, E160B.
Preservatives E210, E211, E220, E250, E251.
Antioxidants E320, E321.

This is not a complete list, so if you have any concerns about additives go to www.bryngollie. freeserve.co.uk.

The Food Standards Agency publishes a free booklet listing all the E numbers to watch out for and why.

Why buy organic?

After months of feeding your mite a liquid lunch (and dinner and breakfast and afternoon tea!), watching them taste their first mouthful of solid food is as monumental a moment as their first word or step. Just as walking and talking require special nurturing and support, making sure your child develops a positive relationship with food is a fundamental responsibility of being a parent. You might assume feeding and watering your young one can't be too difficult (most people do it, don't they?), but with childhood obesity on the rise, increasing concerns about allergies and the mounting evidence linking poor diet with bad behaviour, it's time to make some important decisions.

You might encounter a bit of a minefield of contradictory information while choosing the right food for your baby. The first major choice is the one between organic or non-organic. You're probably familiar with the organic sections in the supermarket and in the increasing number of health-food shops. You've probably also noticed that organic produce is more expensive, goes off quicker and the colour and shape often don't compare to non-organic. So why bother?

What price health?

The price we pay for slightly cheaper non-organic vegetables is chemicals. There are almost 3,000 of them in our food chain. Conventional farming regularly uses a cocktail of chemicals to kill weeds, insects and other pests to meet the tough cosmetic standards and a uniformity of size dictated by the chain stores. Take the common Cox's apple. You might think this is the perfect dessert, gently cooked, for your newly weaned baby, but just one apple could be sprayed up to 16 times with 36 different pesticides.

That's a problem because babies are even more susceptible to chemical residues than the average adult simply because they have a much higher intake of food and water per unit of body weight. Also, their tiny, immature digestive and immune systems mean they have a very limited ability to detoxify any chemical substances.

Organic foods are free from pesticide contamination because synthetic chemicals in organic farming are banned, so I recommend using organic fruit and veg especially for children under 1 year of age – when they are at their most vulnerable. Although regulations for babyfood manufacturers are extremely strict when it comes to micro-biological and chemical testing, I take the view that if the produce is organic it won't have chemicals at all instead of relying on chemical testing for known chemicals. Consider the Olympics and how athletes can get round the rules and you'll see why I believe chemical testing is a safeguard but not an absolute. For me it's just not worth the risk.

Lifestyle choice

Beyond the food safety issue, there is the added bonus of supporting a way of farming that is not damaging the environment. Organic farming produces foods in fields that have been free from contaminants for a minimum of 3 years, rather than doctored with a cocktail of chemicals. And if all this is making you feel pretty good about yourself you'll be chuffed by the end-result in your shopping basket as organic food usually has a far superior taste, texture and flavour to its non-organic rival.

Quick-reference nutrition guide

Get yourself a cup of tea, because as they say in the shampoo commercials this is the science bit. Certain foods are important for your child's development and will help you to give your baby a balanced but varied diet. You may be able to reach for a choccie bar or a packet of crisps when you're peckish but unfortunately going dietary off-piste with your baby will lead to a seriously bumpy downhill run. So pay attention!

I've given a few examples of good food sources for each nutrient to help illustrate, though not all foods are suitable for a young baby. See page 21 and also each chapter for when to introduce what to your baby.

Carbohydrates

Or carbs, as they are now affectionately called in the post-Atkins era. We derive our energy and warmth from carbohydrates. When eaten they are broken down into glucose, which is carried to the muscles, brain and other organs to enable us to function. Children need about five portions of carbohydrates a day and these should form about two-thirds of their diet.

Watch out, though, because there are bad carbs (simple carbs) and good carbs (complex carbs). Just imagine the story of the hare and the tortoise.

The hare and the tortoise

Simple carbs (the hare) include sugar, are most commonly found in refined foods (think cakes, white bread, biscuits). They give a short, intense energy burst that disappears just as rapidly, leaving you craving more.

Complex carbs (the tortoise) include unrefined flours, grains, pulses, fruit and veg. Because they are slower to digest than simple carbs, they release energy over a longer, more sustained period.

If your child eats too many simple carbs, their energy levels will yo-yo throughout the day. The refining process used to manufacture many of these carbs also strips foods of their vitamins and minerals. Take, for example, zinc, found in the outer layer of grain; if it's refined, the outer layer is stripped taking with it this valuable nutrient.

Food sources

Simple carbs cakes, white bread, white pasta, sweets, white rice (see also section on sugar below).

Complex carbs vegetables, fruit, grains, pulses including lentils, wholemeal flour, oats, rye or wholegrain bread, brown pasta, brown and wild rice (see also section on fibre on pages 17–18).

Fats

Fat has had a bad press. We all know we shouldn't eat too much but we (and children especially) need to have fat of the right type and in the right amounts in our diets. Our bodies without fat are similar to a car grinding to a halt without oil; we need a small amount of certain fats to provide the essential lubricants that make us run smoothly inside and out.

Fats also go hand in hand with vitamins A, D, E and K and minerals such as calcium.

Like carbs, there is 'good' fat and 'bad' fat:

Monounsaturated and polyunsaturated fats The good cops. As a rule of thumb you can recognise these as liquid at room temperature. Typically they are derived from fish, nuts, seeds, fruit and vegetables. These essential fats are made up of essential fatty acids and are called essential because they are essential for life but can't be made by our own bodies.

Omega fatty acids

I'll give a special mention to the Omega fatty acids: Omega 3, Omega 6 and their less well-known cousin Omega 9. All are essential to life, but 3 and 6 can only be derived by eating foods containing them. Omega 9 can be produced by our bodies, though an additional supply from our diet is considered advisable. They all play an important role in our bodies whether we are children or adults, being necessary for supple skin, the development of the brain, growth of the nervous system and of muscle, protection from cancers... the list goes on.

For children, Omega 3 is very important for brain development, improving the ability to concentrate. A recent study amongst primary-school children in the UK who were given Omega 3 supplements in their diets saw a remarkable change in school performance with concentration levels improving by 35 per cent.

Our diets tend to provide a plentiful supply of Omega 6 oils but lack Omega 3. The ideal ratio of Omega 6 to Omega 3 fats is 5:1 but ratios of Omega 6 to Omega 3 can be as imbalanced as 50:1.

Saturated fats The bad cops. As a quick rule of thumb they are recognisable as being solid at room temperature and typically come from animals (in meat or dairy) – though coconut and palm oil are also high in saturated fats.

Some saturated fat is good for children, especially as a warming extra energy source for the winter months. Too much will solidify in the body and clog up arteries and form hard-to-shift stores, in clumps around the body. Nice. Although they provide an energy source, what makes them particularly nasty is the way they compete with the good cops, reducing the absorption of the essential oils.

Food sources

Monounsaturated and polyunsaturated fats oils from olives, avocados, fish, seeds (for older children, nuts).
Omega 3 fatty acids are most readily found in fish, particularly oily fish (e.g. salmon, trout, mackerel, sardines, tuna). Some organic hens are now being fed a diet high in Omega 3 – providing organic free-range eggs and chickens

richer in Omega 3 than average – particularly handy if your child dislikes oily fish. If you are choosing a vegetarian diet for your baby you need to be particularly mindful of alternative Omega 3 sources: tofu, linseed oil (flaxseed), ground linseed and for an older child, sunflower seeds, pumpkin seeds, sesame seeds and walnuts. See also Vegetarian babies on page 82.
Omega 6 fatty acids almonds, pine nuts, avocados, corn, sunflower seeds, soya.
Omega 9 fatty acids olive oils, avocados, some nut oils.
Saturated fats include red meat, butter, dairy products and cheeses. They provide a good source of energy, but compete for absorption with the essential oils.

Proteins

Without proteins, we would be jelly. Proteins help to develop our skeletons and muscles as we grow and maintain our body tissues. They also act as messengers between the brain, nervous and hormonal systems. Initially children need more protein per kilo of body weight than a fully grown adult. Proteins are broken down into amino acids in the digestive tract then dispersed around the body to help build and rebuild every cell in our body. Proteins are made up of 22 amino acids, 8 of which are 'essential' (we don't make them ourselves so we need to eat them). Meat, fish and dairy contain the full spectrum of amino acids we need; however it is harder work to get the full amino acid set if you're a vegetarian.

Food sources

Meat, poultry, fish, dairy as well as eggs, seeds, grains especially quinoa, beans and pulses including lentils, soya and soya-based foods such as tofu. Nuts are also protein-rich but can be allergenic: see Avoiding allergies, pages 56–7.

Fibre

Fibre, along with the right amount of fluid, keeps food on the move through your bowels. Most adults could do with increasing the amount of fibre they eat, while older children also need a fibre-rich diet instead of one based on refined foods because without it our systems become sluggish and constipated. However, roughage can be too coarse for a baby's bowels and that's why early weaning foods are peeled and cooked: it's the peel rather than the flesh of fruit and veg that contains the most roughage.

There are two types of fibre, both of which are needed to keep things moving:

Insoluble fibre (also called roughage) helps to sweep the colon and is important in adults and older children. Young bowels can find these abrasive.

Soluble fibre maintains some bulk in the bowels: see Poo, page 29.

Food sources

Insoluble fibre wheat and other grain husks, oats, skin of fruit and vegetables, unrefined (brown) flour, rice, pasta.
Soluble fibre fruits, vegetables, beans and pulses.

Sugars

Sugar is a simple carbohydrate and is a huge issue in children's diets as one of the worst culprits in the obesity epidemic. Why? When your blood sugar goes up, you produce more insulin. And the more insulin you produce, the more sugar you dump as fat. Sugar is very, very addictive and can send moods and energy levels on a rollercoaster ride – the lows causing us to crave more and so the cycle continues. But hold on, sugar is composed of a group of simple carbohydrates and the problem is mainly caused by the kind of sugar that is spooned into and on to food. Soft drinks can contain about 8 teaspoons of refined sugar and most jelly-like sweets are virtually pure sugar – it's highly refined from sugar cane and sugar beet, of little nutritional value and one of the main causes of tooth decay.

Fruit and, to a lesser extent, milk and vegetables contain natural sugars and should provide enough sweetness for adults and children alike. In a child's first year you should not add any extra sugar to their food – just use the natural sweetness of the pure ingredients.

Keep an eye out for added sugars when you're doing your supermarket shop as they are found in many processed foods. Sugars are known by other aliases, including glucose syrup, sucrose, maltose, fructose and dextrose. For more on sugars, see Read the label on page 13.

Honey is seen as a natural alternative to sugar but is a big no-no for babies under 12 months. Never use it to sweeten babyfood – this is not because of nutrition but for food safety reasons. In rare cases, honey can contain spores of the bacteria *Clostridium botulinum*, which can cause serious food poisoning or infant botulinum, a very nasty bacteria that infants are susceptible to. You may find that some commercial babyfood manufacturers use honey to sweeten recipes unnecessarily – they can do this because the extreme temperatures needed to process the food destroys the bacteria but consequently damages the purées' taste, texture and colour.

Salt

Salt is the common name for sodium chloride and is also being eyed up by food experts as a serious player in the rising obesity problem. It may be that high levels of salt make certain foods so more-ish, triggering a reaction in our bodies that makes us crave them. It's notable most junk foods, ready meals and many of our favourite snacks are laden with flavour-enhancing salt.

Salt should never be added to food for a baby under 12 months old as their kidneys are not able to cope with it. All babyfood manufacturers are required to adhere to this advice when formulating their products.

As adults, the amount of salt we like in our food can creep up without us really noticing so as you start to make and taste babyfood you may initially find it bland. Accept that it's salt-free and you might be surprised at how you also start to re-experience the real taste of the pure foods you are preparing. The addition of herbs and spices is a flavoursome alternative to adding salt.

Salt is rarely listed on the labels of foods; instead it will be included under the heading sodium. Sodium occurs naturally in a wide variety of foods and some sodium is essential in the diet, but a normal, mixed diet will provide your infant with all the sodium they require without the need for any added salt.

Vitamins and minerals

Vitamins and minerals are essential for well-being and work quietly behind the scenes to ensure everything is tickety boo. Vitamins are either water soluble (they dissolve in water), like vitamin B and C, or fat soluble (they are stored in the liver and fat tissues of your body), like vitamins A, D, E and K. Water-soluble vitamins travel through your body, coming out in urine, and need to be guzzled daily, while fat-soluble vitamins are stored by the body for up to six months and called on as needed.

Vitamin A (beta-carotene)
What does it do?
Builds good eyesight (helps you to see in the dark), keeps skin soft and smooth, a must for your immune system, needed for gleaming teeth, hair and fingernails and important for maintaining the health of the thyroid gland.
Food sources Orange/red fruit and vegetables, e.g. carrots, red peppers, sweet potatoes, pumpkin and squash, peaches, tomatoes, egg yolk, oily fish, whole milk.

Vitamin B (thiamin, riboflavin, niacin, pantothenic acid, pyridoxine, cyanocobalamin, folic acid)
What does it do?
Vitamin B is actually a group of vitamins (B1, B2, B3, B5, B6, B12, folic acid and biotin). In general terms they help to convert food into energy, keep our stomachs and intestines healthy and help to prevent infections. Specifically, B1 and B2 help to break down food and stave off infection; B3 builds brain cells; B5 helps to maintain red blood cells; B6 helps to produce antibodies to fight disease; B12 is essential for the development of the central nervous system. Folic acid is essential for blood formation, and in pregnancy it helps to prevent neural tube defects, such as spina bifida; also essential for the development of the central nervous system.
Food sources A balanced diet! Whole grains, pulses, green leafy vegetables, dairy, eggs, oily fish, red meat; for older kids: nuts, brewers' yeast and yeast extract – note this is high in salt, so not recommended for those under 12 months.

Vitamin C (ascorbic acid)
What does it do?
Vitamin C helps to fight infection and to absorb iron. It's important for healing, acts as an antioxidant (offers protection against free-radical damage that can precipitate cancer, heart disease and other conditions). It is essential for building muscles and cartilage.
Food sources All fruit (particularly berries, kiwi fruit, citrus fruits, strawberries). All red, green and yellow vegetables (particularly red and yellow sweet peppers, tomatoes and broccoli).

Vitamin D (calciferol)
What does it do?
Helps the absorption of calcium and phosphorus as well as helping to strengthen bones and teeth.
Food sources With the increase in the incidence of skin cancer, many of us are keeping out of the sun; however, a little sun is essential for making vitamin D. If sun is a no go, try oily fish, liver, egg yolk and butter.

Vitamin E
What does it do?
Contains anti-ageing properties, necessary for healthy cell membranes. Also helps to protect certain fatty acids.
Food sources Wheatgerm, avocado, nuts, seeds.

Vitamin K

What does it do?
Helps the blood to clot (which is needed for wounds to heal); essential to build strong bones and prevent heart disease.
Food sources Green leafy vegetables; also manufactured by the body from gut bacteria.

Calcium

What does it do?
Essential for bones and teeth. Breastfeeding women need it in abundance, but keep in mind that it needs vitamin D to be absorbed.
Food sources All dairy foods (particularly hard cheese and milk), lentils, whole small fish, sunflower seeds, green vegetables, mangoes.

Iron

What does it do?
Essential for the formation of red blood cells; low levels of iron result in anaemia (symptoms include tiredness, lethargy, low energy levels, breathlessness, tingling hands). Iron absorption can be increased by 30 per cent if combined with vitamin C-rich foods, but calcium reduces the uptake of iron.
Food sources Kidney, liver, meats, shellfish, egg yolks, dried apricot, prunes, pumpkin seeds, haricot beans, raisins.

Zinc

What does it do?
Helps the formation of many enzymes and proteins as well as moving vitamin A from liver stores into the bloodstream.
Food sources Red meat, eggs, liver, nuts, onions, shellfish, sunflower seeds, wheat germ, whole wheat.

When to introduce certain foods into your baby's diet

Stage 1 should not be started before 4 months (see note below), stage 2 should not be started before 6 months, stage 3 is for 9 months and onwards and stage 4 for 12 months and onwards.

	Pre-Weaning	Stage 1	Stage 2	Stage 3	Stage 4
Vegetables	No	Peeled, cooked and puréed until smooth – see stage 1 recipes.	Peeled, cooked and puréed with texture – see stage 2 recipes.	Cooked and raw finger foods.	
Fruit	No	Peeled, cooked and puréed until smooth – see stage 1 recipes.	Peeled, cooked and puréed with some texture – see stage 2 recipes. Some raw purées.	Cooked and raw finger foods.	
Milk and Dairy	Breast or formula milk will remain important throughout the first year.		Add towards end of stage: cooked milk, yogurts, hard-boiled eggs, hard cheese.		After 12 months, whole pasteurised milk to drink.
Fish	No	No	Introduce towards the end of this stage. Not smoked.		
Smoked Fish	No	No	No	No	In moderation.
Shellfish	No	No	No	No	Only if well cooked.
Gluten	No	No	No	In moderation.	
Meat and Chicken	No	No	Towards the end of this stage (avoiding high salt e.g. bacon, ham).		
Berries	No	No	Can be introduced if mashed or puréed. Monitor for any reactions.		
Sugar and Artificial Sweeteners	No	No	No	No	If foods need to be sweetened use fruit purées from stage 1.
Fibre (High)	No	No	No	No	As part of a balanced diet.
Salt	No	No	No	No	Food contains salt, so no need to add extra.
Tofu	No	No	Towards the end of this stage.		
Nuts	No	No	No	No	Avoid whole nuts (choking hazard). Introduce ground or as a paste. Monitor for any reactions.
Citrus	No	No	No	Can be introduced.	
Honey	No	No	No	No	After 12 months.

- The Department of Health recommends exclusive breastfeeding for the first 6 months. If you want to start weaning earlier than 6 months you must consult a health visitor or a GP. Weaning earlier than 4 months is known to be detrimental to the health of a baby.
- If your family has a history of allergies to certain foods, you should avoid introducing them until you have consulted a health visitor.

Cooking and storing

Once you get started you'll soon discover that there is a basic pattern to the recipes, especially in the early stages. This is an overview of the method and a quick explanation as to why you're doing what.

Wash Fruit and veg (especially root vegetables) need a good clean if you're using non-organic produce as they are the most susceptible to contamination from chemicals and pesticides. Because organic produce is not allowed to be sprayed you may find the odd insect, especially in broccoli and cauliflower.

Peel This is important because too much roughage can be too harsh on their developing internal system. The skins are also the most exposed to contamination by handling so peeling is a good safeguard in the first two stages.

Chop The secret to a tasty end-result, especially in the early stage purées, is in the size of the pieces. If they vary or are too big, they will end up overcooked. I recommend a 3mm (⅛in) dice for most fruit and veg. Use immediately after chopping as the nutrients start to deteriorate.

Cook Steaming retains the natural flavours and textures of the ingredients. Adding food to boiling water, rather than cooking from cold, also staves off nutrient deterioration. Certain meals and fruits and vegetables lend themselves to pan cooking but you can adapt most of the recipes to the cooking utensils you have in your kitchen.

Blend This enables you to control the textures you give to your baby, which is extremely important in the first two weaning stages. Watch out for potatoes: they need only a quick blitz or the starches come out and make purées gluey, which is why some parents prefer to serve as a mash.

Sieve In the early stages, pushing the purée through a sieve using the back of a spoon, or using a fine mouli will give you a very smooth end-result. Once through this initial stage you can use a coarser plate, which will give you a thicker texture without the worry of any choking hazards sneaking through. Watch out for bananas as they'll end up as a grey sludge if you try to sieve them.

Cool Always allow the food to cool, and then test it yourself to make sure it is the right temperature to serve to your baby. If you want to store some of the food in the fridge or freezer, cover and cool first as heat can reduce the efficiency of your fridge or freezer. Don't leave food out at room temperature, especially rice, meats and fish, as this is the most dangerous for producing bacteria (see page 27 for details on freezing).

Equipment

If you've ever been to a baby show, you'll have seen the huge array of products available for kitting out your baby. Now there are parents whose priority is to dress their mini-me head to toe in Gucci (good on them), but parents should also appreciate that food is crucial at all stages of development so getting the right equipment to encourage your child along is imperative. You may already have some of this equipment in your kitchen, but here are a few pointers to help you choose what to buy.

For babies

Weaning spoons Metal conducts heat, so always choose a plastic spoon, preferably one with a long handle and a shallow bowl with blunt sides.

Weaning bowls Look out for small, plastic bowls. Try a bowl with two compartments so you can put carrot purée in one side and apple in the other and mix the two together as the meal goes on. Or try one food you know they eat and introduce a new one.

Bibs Draping a clean-tea towel is equally effective as a cotton bib. For trainee spoon users, a plastic bib with a trough will help to catch bits. Bibs with a plastic backing will protect clothes from getting wet or stained.

Bouncy chair or Bumbo In the first stages of weaning before your baby is ready for a high chair, use a bouncy chair or a plastic Bumbo chair to support their back. It will also keep your hands free.

High chair If your baby has full head control and a strong back, it's time for a high chair. High chairs that can be pulled right up to the table and be adjusted as your child grows are the best. Chairs like this make them feel part of the whole mealtime gig. They love it. Ensure they are safely fastened in so they can't wriggle and fall out. Some babies get fed up with being in the chairs for too long, so don't hoist them up until the meal is ready.

For toddlers

Toddler-friendly cutlery Choose varieties with a short handle that is easy to hold (some come with grips). Novelty train and aeroplane spoons are a cunning idea and will help to distract fussy feeders.

Toddler plates You can buy ones that come with individual compartments, which can appeal to picky eaters as well as create a come-hither-looking meal, or you can just use toddler-friendly non-divided plates. Some plates come with a funny picture – an incentive for your child to get to the bottom of the food.

For the kitchen

Ice-cube trays and mini-freezer pots These are a must. When you've made your purée, simply portion it into the pots or trays and use as needed. Cover ice-cube trays with a freezer bag before freezing. You can re-use Fresh Daisy containers and some yogurt pots (sterilise them first, see page 26). When using plastic cups or ice-cube trays, make sure they are sealed tight as they can be contaminated by other products in the freezer.

Small freezer bags and a marker pen Decant the frozen cubes into small, single-serving bags and mark with the purée variety and date so you can easily identify them later.

Hand-held electric blender These are a God-send; seek out an electric blender pack which includes a small chopping bowl and blade as these are fantastic for tiny stage 1 quantities and getting a very smooth texture. As your child gets older you can simply purée cooked vegetables in the saucepan (and economise on dishes).

Food-processor Although these are rarely able to create very fine purées for fledging foodies, food-processors are handy for stage 2 purées. They come into their own for fine-chopping large quantities quickly.

Mouli This is a food mill you turn by hand (see photograph left), particularly good for giving stage 1 purées a reassuring final sieve. It's ideal for tough-skinned foods, such as prunes, dried apricots, peas and broad beans, as it produces an even purée by keeping out coarse fibrous parts (like husks or skins).

Electric steamer An electric steamer with timer switch and stock-collecting tray (see photograph above) will save you time, deliver the best flavour and, unlike a saucepan, they don't have to be watched in case they boil over. I'm a big fan.

Chopping boards Raw meat and fish should have a separate board from cooked. Rather than clutter up your kitchen, check out small dishwasher-friendly chopping boards, in different colours to help you to remember which one is for what.

Hygiene and sterilisation

Food hygiene for babies

When it comes to preparing food for babies, cleanliness is next to godliness. If you've been a slob in your pre-baby existence, now is the time to shape up – you might be able to withstand the bacteria of week-long leftovers but your baby will not. Their immune system is only just developing and needs you to take extra care and attention in the kitchen. A bout of food poisoning could make them very ill indeed. So get out the mop, throw away those mangy old dishcloths and swot up on a few golden rules.

The fridge

Make sure the fridge temperature is set between 1 and 5°C and the freezer should be no warmer than -18°C. (Fridge and freezer thermometers are available from most department stores.)

Store your baby's food (and bottles) in the middle of the fridge. Avoid the door compartment as it is the warmest part of the fridge and the very back as it can be cold enough to freeze.

Always put raw meat at the bottom of the fridge, so that the juices can't drip down and contaminate other food in the fridge.

Sterilising and cleaning

Now that every stray toy, book or shoe is heading straight for your baby's mouth, there's not much point in sterilising anything other than their eating and drinking utensils (console yourself with the knowledge that babies need a few germs to build up their defences). What you can do is:

Wash all baby's plates and utensils in the dishwasher on the hottest cycle or invest in a pair of rubber gloves and wash in very hot water, then rinse in clean water, ideally over 60°C (140°F), and air dry.

Regularly mop the floors and wipe down the high chair before and after every meal.

Clean all surfaces using a non-toxic sterilising fluid diluted according to the manufacturer's instructions – there are several brands available already diluted in handy spray bottles for added convenience and speed.

Don't skimp on dishcloths – dirty damp cloths can spread bacteria through the kitchen. Wash them regularly on the hottest machine setting or use disposable cloths and throw them away.

Change your tea-towels every day or more often if dirty.

Preparing food

By following a few guidelines, you'll know that your baby (or your kitchen floor, at least) is getting both the freshest and healthiest food there is.

Wash your hands with soap before starting (15 seconds under warm, running water is a good guideline).

Use separate boards for cutting meat and vegetables – ideally rigid plastic ones. Don't use wooden ones as they are porous and retain bacteria. Scrub them down in hot water after use and allow to air dry.

Wash fruit and vegetables thoroughly and peel if they are not organic as this will protect your baby against pesticides.

Freezing, defrosting and reheating

If you are freezing babyfood, small bags are best as they are sealable. If you are using ice-cube trays be extremely careful as leaving them uncovered in the freezer leaves them open to contamination from the other products being stored. Check out the fab individual cube moulds with lids (see photograph right).

Always label and date food so you know what it is and when it needs to be thrown away (fruit, veg and meat purées can be kept for up to 3 months; fish, grains and pulses for 2).

Reheat food until it is piping hot, then allow to cool before serving to your baby. Always be very careful with rice. If left for several hours at room temperature, cooked rice can cause food poisoning. Further cooking or reheating will not destroy the bacteria. Either keep rice hot (at or above 63°C/145°F) or refrigerated or frozen. If using baby rice always make small amounts fresh each time as you require.

Do not reheat foods more than once and never refreeze uneaten food.

ABOVE RIGHT: Beetroot purée, see page 66

Finger foods

Life will get easier as your baby starts to eat more of what you do but there are still a few rules to remember:

Never leave food in open tins. Transfer leftovers into a closeable container, store in the refrigerator and eat within 48 hours.

Babies are particularly susceptible to salmonella, so cook eggs until the white and yolk are solid.

Don't offer a medium-rare option – cook all meat until the juices run clear.

Look at the use-by date on all products.

And finally, if you're concerned about any food for any reason DON'T GIVE IT TO YOUR BABY!

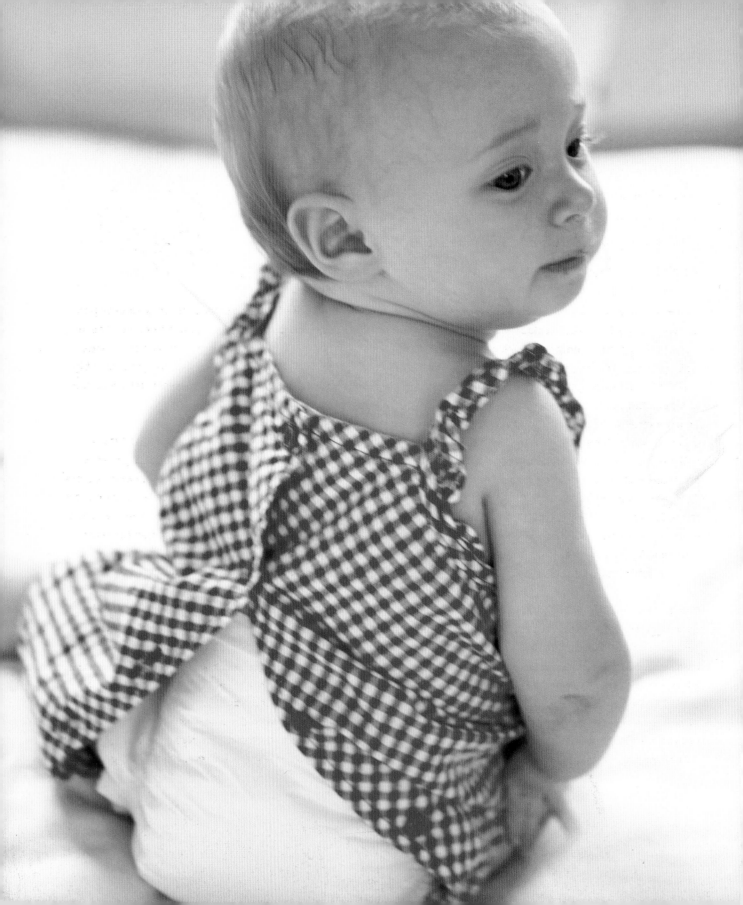

Poo

OK, stop sniggering, we all do it (yes, even the Queen) and when it comes to your child (and even you) it's a great way of checking to see if everything is working properly. Think of your baby as a little production unit. If food passes through their system too quickly (diarrhoea) or slowly (constipation) then the unit is not going to operate properly and your baby is not getting the best out of their food. So have your clipboard at the ready and put your supervisor's hat on because here's a quick guide to poo. Bet they didn't teach you about this at school!

As you start to wean your baby, you'll soon notice that their poo will change drastically in colour and smell from the mustard-colour of milk-only poo to the more 'human-looking' logs.

When first weaning, your baby may find some foods hard to digest. And because you're feeding one vegetable at a time (for example beetroot), you may find their poo will be coloured like the food (a beetroot eater's poo can be very red). Don't be alarmed – it's perfectly natural (but a bit of a nightmare on the nappies!).

Your baby may find it hard to pass some of their first foods. Baby rice, for example, can clog up little bowels, as can bananas. If your baby is really straining (going red in the face, eyes bulging, even crying) you may need to alter their diet and liquid intake.

Helping things along

Ways to prevent poo from being too dry and hard is to give your baby more fruit (particularly pears) or boiled water (in a beaker or bottle) when feeding. Prune purée (see page 74), served alone or mixed in with fruit or baby rice or diluted prune juice is another way of gently getting those bowels to work. Hard poo may be a sign that your baby is not getting enough to drink: add a little formula or breast milk or cooking water to loosen their food – and bowels –

up. To help the elimination process, ensure your baby gets some exercise each day as being stuck in a pram for too long can also jam them up. When 'exercising' take their nappy off and let them kick around under a baby gym or on a big mat with toys just out of reach or put them on their tummy for a bit.

Speeding things up or slowing them down

If your toddler is constipated, it may be that they need to eat a little more fibre, so swap white bread for brown, white pasta for wholemeal, and include fibre-filled beans or lentils until the problem has resolved itself. If all else fails a burst of exercise and fresh air (travel, change, illness and stress are clogging culprits) may do the trick.

Diarrhoea is another issue, but the causes can be quite varied. It can be related to an illness, a food sensitivity or an indication that your baby is eating too much fruit or fibre. Tiny tots can get dehydrated very quickly so ensure they keep up their fluid intake with diluted non-citrus fruit juice. If the diarrhoea is really bad, you may need oral rehydrating salts available from your chemist; ask your pharmacist or doctor for advice. After a bout of diarrhoea, give your little one food that is easy to digest and kind on the gut; for example rice, banana, toast, pear purée, sweet potatoes and live natural yogurt (this helps to rebuild lost gut flora).

Tastes from day one

A healthy, protein-packed diet will help you cope during this energy-sapping stage and give breastfeeding babies a taste of things to come.

Milk, milk, glorious milk

There's no escaping from it and here it comes again in big bold letters: breast is best. Breast milk provides your baby with all their nutritional needs. Yes, your milk is perfectly concocted for your baby. The benefits of breastfeeding are endless. From the gold-top first milk of colostrum – high in protein, vitamins, minerals and antibodies – to your silver-top everyday breast milk, your own milk changes with your baby's needs. And, what's more, as you vary what you eat, it comes in a variety of flavours (and even colour tints) too.

Breastfeeding

A varied, nutritious diet helps to create a good milk supply and also lays the foundation for your baby's tastebuds. The good news is you don't have to follow the perfect diet to produce great milk. Nature is fabulously forgiving. Women in famine conditions produce perfectly good breast milk, but eventually the body draws on its own reserves, which can result in deficiencies for the mother. In general, mineral levels (iron, copper, chromium, zinc) are stable in human milk regardless of maternal blood levels.

Eating for two

To maintain an abundant supply of milk, most women need around 1,800–2,200 calories a day. If you consume less, your milk supply could drop. On average, an exclusively breastfeeding mother needs to consume about 300–500 calories a day more than she used to before her pregnancy. Most women put on lovely maternal fat stores during pregnancy which contribute about 200 extra calories a day towards lactation, so it may be that you only need one or two extra snacks a day.

So what food should you avoid? Although advice will say you can include all the things you've put a hold on while pregnant, overdoing the rich foods may make your baby colicky. If your own or your partner's family has an allergy history with a certain food, avoid them – if in any doubt, nuts and especially peanuts could also be worth avoiding (see pages 56–7).

If you are having a go at breastfeeding but finding it harder than you expected, you're not alone. Talk to your health visitor – there are some fantastic breastfeeding counsellors you can be referred to. For everything you need to know about breastfeeding, go to the National Childbirth Trust website: www.nationalchildbirthtrust.co.uk or breast-feeding experts at www.la.lecheleague.co.uk.

First tastes for your baby

Your newborn baby cries, whimpers, grizzles as they shout, 'Fill me up, Mum', at every starter, breakfast, lunch, dinner and midnight snack. Milk is all your baby wants – and, in the early months, it's all your baby needs.

Yet these months are more than just a milky whitewash and your little gourmet is forming taste preferences before they even have a tooth. That means, and it's a biggie, everything, yes everything you eat while breastfeeding is influencing your baby's taste preferences. Research has shown that a baby's tastebuds may even be shaped in the womb by the flavour of your amniotic fluid, which acts as a 'flavour bridge' to breast milk.

Breast milk is also a 'flavour bridge' to food and, depending on what you eat, your milk will come in an array of mouth-watering flavours. This isn't a new discovery. Medical documents from as far back as the 14th century state that a mother's milk could be more pleasant if the mother ate sweet foods or imbibed fragrant wines (presumably in moderation!). On the other hand, salty or seasoned meats and particular spices would cause her milk to become 'heated' and 'acrimonious'.

In 2004, a research study at the Monell Institute in Philadelphia showed that breastfed babies with mothers who have a varied diet are much more likely to accept unfamiliar flavours when weaned and are more willing to try new vegetables than their formula-fed friends. Another study showed that when garlic flavours are present in breast milk, babies are inclined to suck for longer, but when alcohol is present, they suck more quickly initially, but drink less and finish faster. As you breastfeed you may find your baby relishes some flavours and rejects others. Watch what you eat, then see how long they suck for – keep an eye out for foods that could make your milk bitter as babies innately reject bitter tastes (it's a lifesaving reflex as many natural poisons are bitter to taste). A hit of strong coffee will flavour your milk within 30 minutes.

Why breast milk is great for your baby

- Breast milk is a nutritionally complete food for your baby.
- Human milk provides your baby's first set of living immune cells.
- Human milk has special ingredients, e.g. DHA (docosohexaenoic acid) and AA (arachidonic acid), which contribute to brain and eye development.
- Breast milk gives your baby the first tastes of real food.
- Mothers who breastfeed for 6 months have a reduced risk of breast cancer.
- Mothers who breastfeed lose their maternal fat stores quicker than those who bottlefeed.

Bottlefeeding and formula milk

Before formula, the only alternative to breast milk was another mother's milk. A wet nurse was the only milk substitute. In the Middle Ages it was believed a wet nurse's vices could be sucked through their milk so candidates were always carefully selected – hair colour, for example, was then viewed with suspicion. Animal milk wasn't even considered until the 18th century, for if a child's temperament could come from a human's milk, just imagine what kind of characteristics they might inherit from a cow. In fact, normal cow's milk is too high in protein and salt to be used without modification in any infant under a year.

These days formula milk manufacturers give cow's milk a human-friendly makeover to make it suitable for babies under 1 year, by modifying the carbohydrates, proteins and fats in animal milk and adding vitamins and minerals including folic acid, zinc and iron.

Alternatives to dairy formula milk

The alternatives to milk formula include soya-bean-based formula, but this is not recommended for babies under 6 months. Lactose intolerance in babies is rare, but signs to watch out for include abdominal pain and swelling, gas and diarrhoea. If your baby is experiencing these symptoms seek medical advice for alternative formulas – these will usually only be available on prescription.

Choose organic

When selecting formula, check the labels and choose organic formulas whenever you can. The formulas are made from cows that haven't been given growth hormones and are reared in organic meadows, so the milk is less likely to carry harmful chemical or pesticide residues. As always, keep everything pristine clean as milk is a fertile breeding ground for bacteria. When you use new bottles, rings or teats, always sterilise them first.

The big breakfast

Lunch may be for wimps but breakfast is a meal even Sylvester Stallone would struggle to do without. Skipping breakfast, then running on empty will result in a serious breakdown before lunchtime and just so we know where we stand, three strong coffees, back to back, do not constitute a healthy breakfast! These days breakfast is more likely to be a quick fill-'er-up on the run, rather than a relaxed lie in with a newspaper and a pot of tea but if you choose simple, easy-to-prepare meals you can eat all the energy-packed foods you need to get you through the day.

Having your breakfast on a silver tray is probably restricted to a time your partner is trying to get out of the dog house but one thing remains a constant and that's the importance of a good breakfast. Those who eat a proper breakfast work faster, make fewer mistakes, suffer fewer colds and have a better short-term memory. What's more, they are less likely to have vitamin or mineral deficiencies.

Without breakfast, hunger levels soar and energy levels plummet by mid-morning, which is when we reach for high-energy foods or overindulge at lunchtime. Skipping breakfast means you are more likely to have a higher body mass index.

Food for the brain

Breakfast is also vital brain fodder. Researchers in Scotland found that consuming a breakfast rich in complex carbohydrates benefits short-term memory by supplying the brain with a steady supply of glucose. Children who eat a breakfast rich in complex carbs improved their memory performance throughout the morning. Researchers from the USA found that children who don't eat breakfast have problems with basic problem-solving skills, verbal fluency and the ability to recall facts.

What is a good breakfast?

What to eat? We all bow to Maximilian Bircher-Benner, the creator of 'Birchermüsli' at his Living Force Clinic in 1900. His cereal, made originally from grated apple, lemon juice, milk and nuts and grains, was 'prescribed' as a protection against illness of all kinds (this is now backed up by a study from the University of Wales, which reveals that those who eat breakfast are less likely to suffer from colds and flu). Muesli is probably the only Swiss-German word to have gone global. It's a meal in one, loaded with vitamin C (fresh fruits), calcium (yogurt, milk), protein (nuts or seeds), iron (dried apricots and prunes) and more. Not only is it lovely with milk, you can also turn it into crumble topping or create nutritious snacks like flapjacks or muffins for your toddlers.

Full Monty Muesli – Real Swiss Style

The original Birchermüsli, though wholesome, could also be described as a bit too worthy. These days if you ask for a Birchermüsli you can expect a delicious fruity, yogurty, oaty bowl of loveliness that will fill you up and feel like a treat without the guilt trip of a full English.

Makes 1 serving (not suitable for freezing)

THE NIGHT BEFORE
1 tablespoon rolled oats
3 tablespoons water

JUST BEFORE SERVING
1–2 tablespoons yogurt, cream or crème fraîche
1 apple
1 tablespoon mixed berries and currants (fresh or, if out of season, frozen)
1 piece of seasonal fruit, e.g. peach, apricot, pear
1 tablespoon lemon juice
1 tablespoon chopped seeds or nuts (traditionally hazelnuts)

Soak the oats in the water overnight – it makes them easier to digest.

Shortly before serving, mix the oats with the yogurt, cream or crème fraîche. Wash, core and grate the unpeeled apple and chop the other fruits as necessary. Stir into the mix. If you like, toast the seeds and nuts (if you are not allergic) and sprinkle on to the mix.

Serve immediately.

Tropical Porridge

This is a tropical version although the same method works with more locally available seasonal fruit. Two brazil nuts a day provide the recommended daily allowance of the mood-enhancing mineral selenium – though omit if you are adapting this recipe for a child.

Makes 1 serving (not suitable for freezing)

125ml (4fl oz) milk
25g (1oz) rolled oats (about a handful)
1 tablespoon dried or fresh mango, papaya and pineapple
1 dessertspoon dried coconut
2 chopped brazil nuts
1 small banana

Pan method

Heat the milk in a small pan and stir in the oats, bring to the boil and return to a simmer.

Stir in the fruit and nuts, if using, and cook for 10–12 minutes until the oats are soft. Pour into a bowl and top with banana – which will help to cool it slightly.

Microwave method (and washing-up-saving method)

Combine all the ingredients except the banana in a large, microwave-safe, breakfast bowl. (Choose a bowl bigger than you think needed as it tends to bubble up and can boil over.)

Cook for 1 minute on full power, stir and leave to stand for 1 minute then cook for another 40 seconds, stir and leave to stand for another minute. Check the oats are soft (if not, give it another 20 seconds on full).

Slice in the banana and allow to cool a little.

Stylish soup

Aah… soup. It's a hug in a bowl. There's nothing quite like cradling a steamy hot bowl of soup in clay-cold hands, aromas drifting nose-height from the kitchen. I just love soup. It can be any flavour you like, creamy, spicy or herby; it's nutritious, a substantial well-balanced meal, quick to prepare and – for the most culinary phobic among you – simple to make.

All you need is a chopping board, a knife and one huge pot and away you go. Simply ladle it into big, generous bowls or mugs (no spoons required) or have it on the run in a large, portable thermos flask.

And add a little extra liquid and your soup will streeettch to feed an army. That's exactly why soup was 'invented' in the 1800s by an Anglo-American, Count Rumford. While in Bavaria he was in a stew trying to figure out how to keep his troops well nourished. 'Soup', his 'discovery' was as exciting as vaccinations or Franklin's lightning bolt. Soup was going to eradicate world hunger.

Count Rumford believed starches – potatoes and barley – would keep his men going for hours. So he threw these two ingredients into an enormous pot and for flavour he added a bucketful of legumes and onion and celery. Before serving, each bowl received a crowning of cheese, fish or meat and a piece of stale bread. His men thrived and the idea spread throughout the armies of Europe. Soup went on to save the lives of thousands in the Great Depression when soup kitchens sprang up to feed the unemployed and destitute. And, even better, soup can save your bacon when you need it too.

Cheesy Broccoli, Cauliflower and Potato Soup

Makes 1 serving

100ml (3½fl oz) water
50g (2oz) broccoli
50g (2oz) cauliflower
50g (2oz) potato
or 7 cubes of frozen Broccoli,
  Cauliflower and Potato
  Purée (see page 87)

25g (1oz) mature cheddar
100ml (3½fl oz) whole milk
Freshly ground black pepper
Small pinch of salt

Bring the water to a rolling boil. Wash and trim the broccoli and cauliflower. Wash and peel the potato, then finely hand chop or run through the grater attachment of a food-processor – the fine chop will speed up the cooking time. Immediately pour the chopped mix into the boiling water and simmer for 5 minutes (for a really speedy option simply defrost 1 pot of Fresh Daisy's stage 2 Broccoli, Cauliflower and Potato Purée in the water).

Grate the cheese and stir in with the milk. Return to a simmer, season and serve.

Sweetcorn Chowder

Makes 1 serving

2 teaspoons olive oil
40g (1½oz) leek
50g (2oz) baby sweetcorn
25g (1oz) peas (fresh or
  frozen)
60g (2½oz) potato
200ml (7 fl oz) whole milk

50ml (2fl oz) water
Freshly ground black pepper
Small pinch of salt
(for a larger meal add 50g
  (2oz) chopped cooked
  chicken or steamed, flaked
  white fish)

Heat the olive oil in a medium saucepan. Finely slice the leek into thin discs and sweat in the olive oil to soften.

Rinse the baby corn and also slice into thin discs; add baby corn and peas to the leeks.

Wash and peel the potato, then cut into small cubes (approx 5mm (¼in). Add the potato, milk and water and boil, then simmer for 10 minutes until the potato is soft.

If you prefer a thick smooth soup rather than chunky, blend with a hand blender (adding the optional fish or chicken). Season and serve.

Carrot, Sweet Potato, and Coriander Soup

Makes 1 serving

2 teaspoons olive oil
¼ medium onion
75g (3oz) carrot
75g (3oz) sweet potato
or 7 cubes of frozen Carrot
  and Sweet Potato Purée
  (see page 86)
100ml (3½fl oz) whole milk

100ml (3½fl oz) water
Freshly ground black pepper
Small pinch of salt
1 dessertspoon freshly
  chopped coriander

Heat the olive oil in a medium saucepan. Finely chop the onion and sauté until soft but not browned. Wash, peel and finely chop or grate the carrot and sweet potato and sauté

for a further 2–3 minutes or add the frozen purée to defrost, stirring continuously.

(For a really speedy option simply warm one pot of Fresh Daisy's stage 2 Carrot and Sweet Potato Purée with the sautéed onion.)

Add the milk and water and bring to a simmer.

Liquidise with a hand blender, season and add the coriander. For an extra treat swirl through a dessertspoonful of crème fraîche.

Spicy Bean Soup

Makes 1 serving

¼ onion
1 garlic clove
2 teaspoons olive oil
75g (3oz) tomatoes (fresh or
  tinned plum tomato)
1cm (½in) cube of fresh
  ginger, peeled and grated or
  ¼ teaspoon dried ginger
150ml (¼ pint) tomato juice
  or 150ml (¼ pint) water and
  ½ tablespoon tomato purée

150g (5oz) tinned mixed
  beans
Pinch of cayenne pepper or
  2–3 drops Tabasco
1 teaspoon Worcester sauce
Freshly ground black pepper
Small pinch of salt
1 teaspoon freshly chopped
  chives

Finely chop the onion and crush the garlic.

Heat the olive oil in a medium saucepan and sauté the onion and garlic until soft but not browned.

Chop the tomato and add to the pan with the finely grated ginger, and sauté for a further 2–3 minutes.

Add the tomato juice (or water and tomato purée). Rinse the beans and stir into the soup and season with the cayenne, Worcester sauce, pepper and salt. Bring back to the boil.

Either liquidise with a hand blender or keep it chunky. Add the chives just before serving.

Salads

Hallelujah. Praise the lettuce. The salad just may be the answer to your nutritional prayers. For food in a flash it's easy to toss together a nutrient-packed salad. All you need is fresh ingredients, a big chopping board, a sharp knife and a generously sized salad bowl.

Salads provide you with several of your 5-a-day requirements (remember one portion is equal to one medium fruit or a quarter of a cup of dried fruit). However, what the 5-a-day mantra doesn't stipulate is that you really need a colour mix to get the right range of nutrients too (see A pot of nutritional gold, opposite). It also pays – health- and wallet-wise – to buy local vegetables and fruits in season. The closer you can eat your food to its natural, fresh-from-the-ground state the more nutritious it is likely to be – you don't want it suffering from food miles jet-lag.

When you build your salad, think in terms of a food pyramid. Start with a base layer of fresh green leaves. Next, 'eat with your eye': select an artful, Picasso-like mix of brightly coloured vegetables and fruit. For a slow-releasing energy burn that will last all afternoon, choose a selection of low GI foods, like boiled potatoes in their skins, whole-wheat pasta shells or cooked lentils. Crown your salad with a protein (think chargrilled chicken, ham, cheese, boiled egg, tuna fish, mackerel). The X-factor? Garnish with fresh herbs or toasted seeds.

A pot of nutritional gold

When you choose a rainbow of vegetables and fruits, you get the right balance of vitamins and minerals as well as a range of antioxidants.

Go Green Darker green in fruit and veg signifies extra goodness. Green veg and fruit contain chlorophyll, the plant's way of converting sunlight to energy. Greens have vitamins A, C and E as well as a mix of minerals, but dark greens also contain lutein and indoles, which have antioxidant, health-promoting properties.
Sources: peas, broccoli, green peppers, cucumber, spinach and asparagus.

See Red The natural red blusher in fruit and veg are lycopene or anthocyanins, two antioxidants (these neutralise 'free radicals' or unstable oxygen molecules that can damage cells).
Sources: watermelons, tomatoes, pink grapefruits, red potatoes, red cabbage, beetroots, cherries.

Bright Almighty Orange and yellow fruit or veg is jam-packed full of natural pigments called carotenoids. Adults who eat plenty of veg high in carotenoids significantly reduce their chances of heart attack. Pumpkins, yams, sweet potatoes and carrots are full of beta-carotene (vitamin A) while citrus fruits are full of vitamin C.
Sources: yellow peppers, oranges, apricots, peaches, yellow plums, sweetcorn.

Get the Blues Purple and blue-hued vegetables and fruits are coloured by water-soluble antioxidant pigments anthocyanins and phenolics, which may help to prevent cancer, stroke and heart disease as well as improve our memories.
Sources: beetroot, blueberries, aubergines, grapes, raisins, figs, plums.

All White White fruits and vegetables contain more 'anthoxanthins' as well as health-promoting chemicals such as allicin, reputed to lower cholesterol and blood pressure and reduce risk of stomach cancer and heart disease.
Sources: bananas, cauliflower, garlic, parsnips, onions.

Salmon with Warm Wilted Salad

Makes 1–2 servings

25g (1oz) mixed seeds
   (e.g. sunflower seeds,
   pumpkin seeds)
1 egg
200g (7oz) salmon
½ tablespoon olive oil
2–3 spring onions
100–150g (3½–5oz) salad
   leaves (e.g. baby spinach,
   rocket, watercress)
Choose from a selection of:
½ red pepper
1 small carrot
½ avocado

5–6 button mushrooms
1 small tomato or a few
   cherry tomatoes
TO COAT THE FISH
1 tablespoon wholemeal plain
   flour
teaspoon dried herbs (mixed
   or single, e.g. oregano,
   basil)
Pinch of salt
Fresh ground black pepper
**Up to ¼ teaspoon spice of
   your choice (e.g. paprika,
   ginger, chilli)**

Toast the seeds in a non-stick frying pan (do not add oil,
simply heat the pan and keep the seeds moving). Set aside.
Hardboil the egg, about 5–6 minutes, and cool off in cold
water (to prevent the yolk blackening).

On a dinner plate combine the ingredients for the
coating. Wash and chop the fish into 5cm (2in) squares. Roll
the fish in the seasoned flour mix. Chop the vegetables into
2cm (1in) pieces. Peel and quarter the egg.

Gently heat the olive oil in the non-stick frying pan and
pan fry the salmon for approximately 5 minutes on each side
until golden. Chop the spring onions into 1cm (½in) pieces
and add halfway through the cooking.

Meanwhile arrange the washed salad leaves on a serving
plate and sprinkle with your chosen vegetables.

Place the hot salmon and quartered egg on top of the
salad.

Turn off the heat then pour the vinaigrette into the still
warm pan and stir round to pick up the flavours of the fish
and spring onion. Pour over the salad to wilt the leaves.
Finally top off with the toasted seeds.

Vinaigrette

Makes 2–3 servings

1 tablespoon olive oil
1 tablespoon freshly
   squeezed lemon juice or
   cider vinegar
Choose from a selection of:
1 garlic clove, crushed
1 teaspoon mild mustard, e.g.
   Dijon or wholegrain

2 drops of Tabasco or small
   pinch of mild chilli powder
1 teaspoon fresh chopped
   herbs or pinch of dried herbs
Freshly ground black pepper

For best results, put all the ingredients in a screw-top jar and
shake. The dressing will keep for 2–3 days if chilled.

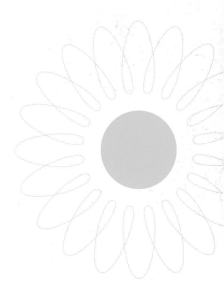

Sorted Caesar

The traditional Caesar Salad can be a simple combination of lettuce, tomato, parmesan and croûtons with or without chicken. My Sorted Caesar adds a few extra ingredients to bring in a few more important colours, giving you a wider range of nutrients.

Makes 1 serving

1 slice multigrain bread	¼ avocado
½ tablespoon olive oil (optional)	2 anchovy fillets
	¼ yellow pepper
1 garlic clove (optional)	¼ red onion
50g (2oz) Romaine or Iceberg leaves	75g (3oz) cooked chicken breast
4–5 cherry tomatoes	15g (¾oz) parmesan cheese

If you like croûtons cut the bread into cubes, heat the oil and garlic in a non-stick frying pan, fry the cubes until golden and set aside to cool. If croûtons are not your thing, simply toast the bread and cut into cubes to give a little crunch to the salad.

Wash and tear the leaves and arrange in a bowl. Wash and slice the cherry tomatoes, avocado, anchovy, pepper and onion, then add to the leaves. Slice the cooked chicken (also works well with lightly smoked trout) and top with parmesan shavings and croûtons or toasted bread cubes.

Drizzle with Simple Caesar Salad Dressing (see below).

Simple Caesar Salad Dressing

Again – not quite the traditional… but quick and delicious.

2 teaspoons fresh lemon juice	1 garlic clove, crushed
2 teaspoons olive oil	Splash Worcester sauce
1 teaspoon Dijon mustard	7–10g (¼–½oz) very finely grated parmesan cheese
1 teaspoon crème fraîche, natural yogurt or mayonnaise	Freshly ground black pepper
	Tiny pinch of salt

Combine all the ingredients in a screw-top jar and shake.

Nuts About Cheese

Two brazil nuts contain an adult's daily requirement of selenium, an important mineral in creating uplifting and positive moods.

If you or your partner have a family history of nut allergies it would be advisable to avoid nuts and sesame seeds if breastfeeding. Sunflower, linseed and pumpkin seeds are known to be less allergenic.

Makes 1 serving

3–4 small salad potatoes	50g (2oz) mixed salad leaves
½ carrot	50g (2oz) goat's cheese
25g (1oz) mangetout	4–5 sun-dried tomatoes
¼ red pepper	25g (1oz) mixed nuts
2 spring onions	

Wash and halve the potatoes and boil or steam until soft. Allow to cool.

Wash, peel and slice the carrot. Wash and slice the mangetout, red pepper and spring onions. Arrange the chopped vegetables and potato on the mixed leaves.

Cut the goat's cheese into cubes and grill until lightly golden, place on the salad with the sun-dried tomatoes and sprinkle with the nuts.

Drizzle with vinaigrette (see page 43).

Bakes

Bakes are great, all-in-one meals, ideal for making in batches then freezing. Defrost overnight in the fridge or on a low (defrost) setting in the microwave then cover and heat through in the oven or microwave. Bakes are particularly warming in winter and fill the house with comforting homely aromas.

Lentil Bake

Makes 1–2 servings

1 dessertspoon olive oil
50g (2oz) onion and/or leek
1–2 garlic cloves
75g (3oz) mushrooms
75g (3oz) sweet potato or squash (butternut or red kuri)
50g (2oz) carrot
50g (2oz) broccoli or spinach
75g (3oz) red lentils
150ml (¼ pint) water or water and milk
1–2 teaspoons fresh mixed herbs or ½–1 teaspoon dried mixed herbs
25g (1oz) sunflower, pumpkin and flax seeds (linseed)
Pinch of cayenne pepper (optional)
Freshly ground black pepper

FOR THE TOPPING
25–50g (1–2oz) wholemeal or wholegrain bread
25g (1oz) hard cheese, grated (optional)

Preheat the oven to 200°C/400°F/gas mark 6.

Lightly toast the bread for the topping and set aside to cool and harden. Heat the oil in a medium saucepan. Peel and roughly chop the onion and/or leek, slice the garlic (it gives a milder taste than crushing) and sauté in the oil for 2 minutes.

Wash, peel and chop the other vegetables and add to the pan. Rinse the lentils and check over for any bits or little stones, then add to the pan. Stir, pour in the water and simmer for 10–15 minutes until the lentils soften but still have a little hardness, adding more water as needed. Add the herbs, seeds and seasoning, then pour the mix into an ovenproof dish.

Crumble the toast – either tear, chop or blitz briefly in a hand blender's chopping attachment – and sprinkle on to the mix and finish off with grated cheese. Bake for 25–30 minutes until the lentils are soft and the topping golden.

Shepherd's Pie

Makes 2–3 servings

250g (9oz) lean mince (traditionally lamb, alternatively beef or turkey)
40g (1½oz) onion
50g (2oz) carrot
1 tablespoon peas (fresh or frozen) or broccoli
1 teaspoon mixed herbs e.g. mint, thyme, marjoram, basil (fresh or dried)
100g (3½oz) tomatoes (fresh or tinned)
Dash of Worcester sauce
Freshly ground black pepper and small pinch of salt (optional)

FOR THE TOPPING
310g (11oz) potato
1 tablespoon milk
10g (½oz) butter
Freshly ground black pepper
25g (1oz) cheese, grated

Preheat the oven to 200°C/400°F/gas mark 6.

Put the mince in a medium saucepan, add the chopped onion and cook until the mince changes colour from red to brown. Keep the mix moving as it cooks; there is likely to be enough fat in the mince without adding any oil, but if it sticks add a little drizzle of olive oil.

Wash, peel and cube or grate the carrot into the mix and stir in the peas and herbs. Chop the tomatoes and stir into the pan with the seasoning, and gently simmer.

Wash, peel and cube the potatoes – smaller cubes will cook quicker. Bring a pan of water to the boil, add the potatoes and simmer or steam until soft. Mash with the milk, butter and pepper.

Spoon the mince mix into an ovenproof dish then layer on the mash, and finally top off with grated cheese. Bake for 30–35 minutes until the cheese bubbles and begins to brown.

Three-Fish Bake

Makes 1 large bake or 2 single bakes

1 egg
400g (14oz) sweet potato
1½ tablespoons olive oil
1 garlic clove, crushed
  (optional)
1 leek, trimmed (100g/3½oz)
  or 1 medium onion
1 medium carrot
½ green pepper
1 teaspoon chopped capers

100g (3½oz) salmon
100g (3½oz) white fish
100g (3½oz) smoked or fresh
  mackerel
1 heaped teaspoon cornflour
200ml (7fl oz) milk
Salt and pepper
A few sprigs of dill
100g (3½oz) broccoli florets
50g (2oz) cheddar cheese

Preheat the oven to 200°C/400°F/gas mark 6.

Hardboil the egg (about 6–7 minutes). Peel and chop the sweet potato. Bring a large pan of water to the boil, add the potato and simmer for 10–15 minutes until the potato has softened. Drain, mash and set aside.

Pour ¼ tablespoon olive oil and garlic, if using, in the bottom of two single-serving ovenproof pie dishes or ½ tablespoon olive oil in one larger ovenproof pie dish. Heat the remaining olive oil in a large frying pan. Chop the leek and sauté. Peel and chop the carrot, dice the pepper and add to the leek with the capers. Gently cook for 5 minutes.

Skin the fish if you prefer, chop into 3cm (¼in) chunks, then chop the boiled egg and add to the frying pan.

Mix the cornflour with a little milk to form a smooth paste then add the rest of the milk. Pour over the fish and veg mixture and stir through. Season with pepper, a small pinch of salt and most of the dill (keep a little to garnish). Cover, bring to a boil and simmer, stirring occasionally.

Divide the mix between the two dishes or put it all in the larger dish. Arrange the broccoli on top and dollop the mash between the florets. Grate the cheese and sprinkle on top.

Bake in the oven for 20 minutes until the topping begins to brown.

If you have made two bakes, enjoy one bake now and allow the other to cool, then freeze. Once frozen you may find that you can release the bake from the pie dish and decant into a freezer bag, thus freeing up the dish for another baking day.

Quick fixes

Are you ready to bite somebody's head off? Dealing with small children is always going to be more *Amityville Horror* than *The Sound of Music* when your system is out of whack. So, stop, get yourself into the kitchen and follow some of the quick-and-easy recipes below. Simply mix up one of the suggested toppings and use on a base of potatoes, egg noodles, wholewheat spaghetti or squash it in between two bits of fresh bread or into a pitta pocket. Your children will notice the change from Frankenstein's monster to Mother Teresa almost immediately.

Creamy Salmon and Dill

Makes 1 serving

50g (2oz) salmon
1 tablespoon crème fraîche
Juice of 1/4 lemon
1/2 teaspoon capers (optional)
1 teaspoon freshly chopped
  dill
Freshly ground black pepper
Pinch of salt
A few spinach or mixed green
  leaves

Steam the fish for 6–8 minutes until it is cooked through. Flake and allow to cool.

Combine the fish, crème fraîche, lemon juice, chopped capers, if using, and dill with a good pinch of fresh ground black pepper and a little salt.

Use with the leaves to top a baked potato, add crunch to a sandwich or you could wilt the leaves by stirring the mix through hot pasta.

Mediterranean Moment

Makes 1 serving

75g (3oz) red, green and
  yellow peppers
2–3 button mushrooms
1/4 courgette
1/2 tablespoon olive oil
1 garlic clove, crushed
50g (2oz) buffalo mozzarella,
  chopped
25g (1oz) sun-dried tomatoes
25g (1oz) olives, stoned
1 teaspoon fresh oregano and
  basil or 1/4–1/2 teaspoon
  dried Italian mixed herbs
1 teaspoon pesto
Freshly ground black pepper

Chop and combine the ingredients (leave out the garlic if you prefer) with a little vinaigrette (see page 43).

Or, heat a ridged griddle pan (or non-stick frying pan). Chop the peppers, mushrooms, and courgette and toss in the olive oil and crushed garlic. Chargrill and remove from the heat.

Sprinkle with the chopped mozzarella, sun-dried tomatoes, olives, herbs and stir in the pesto. Season with pepper. This is a great filling for a ciabatta or jacket potato. It also works very well stirred through hot or cold pasta.

Va Va Voom

Makes 1 serving

1–2 teaspoons toasted linseed, sunflower and pumpkin seeds
50g (2oz) cream cheese or cottage cheese
½ small red onion or 1–2 spring onions
½ beef tomato
50g (2oz) spinach or mixed leaves
Freshly ground black pepper

Toast the seeds in a dry non-stick frying pan (keep them moving to prevent them burning). If time is really short then simply use untoasted.

Stir the seeds into the cheese. Slice the onion and tomato. Wash the leaves.

Layer the ingredients on to a multi-grain bap, or a baked sweet potato. Season and serve.

Zesty Tuna

Makes 1 serving

25g (1oz) mangetout
25g (1oz) baby sweetcorn
1 small tomato
75g (3oz) cooked fresh tuna (or tuna tinned in spring water)
¼ unwaxed lemon
1 tablespoon natural yogurt
A few fresh basil leaves
25g (1oz) cheddar cheese, grated (Optional. You may choose to use less tuna if adding cheese.)
Freshly ground black pepper

Wash and slice the mangetout, baby corn and tomato.

Flake the tuna, zest the lemon and combine with the yogurt.

Layer the tuna mix, baby corn, mangetout, tomato, basil and grated cheese on to fresh bread, baked potato or cold pasta. Season with black pepper.

In colder weather use the mix as a filling for a wholewheat pitta pocket and grill for 3 minutes.

Desserts

Watch your step here because desserts can dazzle you with calories and leave you with little nutrition. Others will take you to the heights of ecstasy only to dump you when they run out of energy. So it's important you're seduced by healthy types who will give you the world of vitamins and minerals. Take, for example, the nicely presented fresh fruit salad. A safe, reliable choice and if you devour a vitamin-C-rich salad after an iron-rich meal you'll maximise your iron uptake – and give yourself more energy.

The way to your nutritional heart should be via a dessert without the sugar daddy sweeteners. Fruit should provide all the sweetness you need. What's more, don't be afraid to let a good-looking, nutrient-laden dessert join you for a great breakfast. An oaty crumble first thing in the morning, heated up from the leftovers of the night before should put a spring in your step for the rest of the day.

You shouldn't have to make something new each time, simply make more than you need and freeze the rest. For example, when you're making a crumble, cook the apples, pears or mango, then freeze a helping to make a base for a crumble in the future. If your baby is coming up to weaning, double your quantities and make single purées for them and grown-up combos for yourself.

Fruit Salad

This is not so much a recipe as a reminder – when choosing fruit, keep the 'Pot of gold' idea for a savoury salad in your mind (see page 41). Keep a multi-coloured fruit bowl on the go and aim for a lidded container of diced fruit salad in the fridge to scoop into breakfast, snack with yogurt or serve as dessert. Liven things up with fresh herbs, such as mint and coriander, and be adventurous – strawberries, for example, are delicious with black pepper and balsamic vinegar.

Oaty Crumble

Makes 2–3 servings

200g (7oz) fruit, e.g. apples, pears, rhubarb, gooseberries, sultanas
¼ teaspoon of spice, e.g. cinnamon, ginger
1 teaspoon brown sugar (optional)

FOR THE CRUMBLE
25g (1oz) butter
25g (1oz) wholemeal plain flour
1 teaspoon brown sugar
40g (1½oz) oats
10g (½oz) mixed seeds, e.g. sunflower, linseeds

Wash and chop the fruit and gently simmer with the spice and sugar, if using, in 1 tablespoon of water until they start to soften (if you like the fruit to have a little bite you could miss out this stage).

Preheat the oven to 200°C/400°C/gas mark 6. Arrange the fruit in a small ovenproof bowl.

To make the crumble, grate the butter into the flour and sugar in a medium mixing bowl and rub in until the mixture resembles breadcrumbs. Stir in the oats and seeds.

Top the fruit with the crumble and bake for 25 minutes or until the crumble begins to brown.

Why not try a tropical crumble? Choose mango, pineapple and banana to make an exotic base, then add coconut flakes and Brazil nuts into the topping.

Baked Apple

Grandma Daisy – the inspiration behind the company name – had apple and plum trees in her garden so baked fruits were a regular treat. Around Christmas time the filling was switched from the dried fruit stuffing in this recipe to home-made mincemeat – delicious but also incredibly quick and easy. This also works with a large pear.

Makes 1 serving

1 teaspoon currants, sultanas or raisins

2 dried apricots (stoned)

2 ready-to eat-prunes or dates (stoned)

Juice of 1/4 lemon

1 teaspoon seeds or nuts (omit if adapting this recipe for a child)

1 cooking apple or large dessert apple (if using cooking apple add 1 teaspoon brown sugar)

10g (1/2oz) butter

Preheat the oven to 200°C/400°C/gas mark 6.

Combine the dried fruit, lemon juice and seeds (and nuts and sugar if using) in the chopping attachment of a hand blender and coarsely chop with a quick blitz.

Wash the apple but do not peel. Use a corer to remove the core – you may wish to core out a little more to fit in more filling. Use a sharp knife and score an incision around the middle of the apple, making sure that you cut through the skin but not deep enough to cut through to the hole in the middle. Place the apple in a small ovenproof dish or mini baking tray.

Push the dried fruit into the hole then top off with the butter – don't worry if there isn't enough room, the melting butter will coat the top of the apple, helping it to go slightly crisp and golden. Bake for 20–30 minutes until you can push a sharp knife easily into the fruit and the top is golden. Serve hot, with a blob of yogurt or crème fraîche if you like.

(Avoid nuts, particularly peanuts, if you or your partner have a family history of nut allergy.)

Baked Banana

OK – we all like chocolate – this ultra-simple recipe combines a way to get one of the 5 fruits a day with a bit of indulgence – and if you choose quality +70 per cent cocoa solid, organic chocolate you will get a mood-enhancing dose of endorphins and serotonin, not just a crash-and-burn sugar hit of lower-quality confectionery.

Makes 1 serving

1 banana

4–5 chunks chocolate

Preheat the oven to 180°C/350°F/gas mark 4.

Don't peel the banana, just use a sharp knife to slice a slit lengthways and slot in the chocolate chunks. Wrap in foil and bake for 20 minutes.

Granita

You'll be making lots of delicious fruit purées for your baby in the next few months – if you have time to make some early, freeze a few cubes then use the rest to treat yourself and your partner to a posh granita.

Makes 1 serving

Approx. 100g (3 1/2oz) fruit purée from stage 1 or 2 (avoid banana and other fruits that don't freeze well)

Add spices of your choice, e.g. cinnamon, cardamom

Pour the purée into a freezable container with a lid. Part freeze for 30–40 minutes to a slush then whisk it up with a fork, repeat the freezing and forking one or two more times until you have fruit ice grains.

Serve in a fancy glass with a sprig of fresh mint.

Stage one:
First steps in weaning

Your child's first encounter with rice, fruit and vegetables. A guide to great first-stage purées and when to introduce them into your baby's diet.

The first stage

How can you tell when your baby is ready for weaning? Your baby will let you know (for more, see the panel on page 56). There's no magic age or weight, but there are physical, emotional and nutritional yardsticks that will indicate it's time to let the puréeing begin.

Like us, all babies are individuals. The key is not to start too soon or too late. Mothers of small babies particularly are often pressured into weaning too early, but the fact is a teaspoon of breast or formula milk contains more calories than a teaspoon of carrots.

Can I wean too soon?

Introducing food too early means that babies run the risk of developing food allergies and intolerances. Why? From birth to 4–6 months of age, babies have what's known as an 'open gut', which means that the spaces between the cells of the small intestines allow food molecules, including whole proteins, to pass directly into the bloodstream. While this is great news for beneficial antibodies in breast milk, it also means that large proteins from other potentially allergy-forming foods can go right through, too. Babies start producing their own antibodies at about 6 months, when the gut 'closes'.

It takes up to 4 months for the lining of the baby's gut to develop and the kidneys to mature enough to cope with the waste products from solid food. If solids are introduced before a baby has a complete set of enzymes required to digest food properly, their digestive system could be damaged. Some digestive enzymes (like gastin and pepsin) reach adult levels around 3–4 months, while starch-busting and carbohydrate-crunching enzymes reach adult levels at around 6 months. Babies have low levels of lipase and bile salts, so fat digestion isn't even considered until around 6 months. Babies are born with a store of iron; however, by 6 months most babies have used up their iron reserves and even if they are drinking iron-fortified milk, it's important to include iron-rich foods.

Even before you start to wean your baby you can get them interested in mealtimes by sitting them with the family. And, yes, they can have their very own breast milk, formula or cooled boiled water. Give your baby spoons, cups, bowls and other utensils to play with or make your own 'mums-icle' (a popsicle made from breast or formula milk).

Do I have to wait 6 months?

You may be aware of the World Health Organisation's guidelines on when to wean. Initially they stated babies should be breastfed exclusively until 6 months. More recent recommendations have clarified weaning should NOT be earlier than 4 months. The introduction of simple fruit and vegetable purées prior to 6 months is only acceptable if the baby is showing the signs of being ready to wean (see panel on page 56).

During the first months of weaning, your baby will need both first-stage purées and breast or formula milk.

I welcome these guidelines as it is all about when your baby is ready and not when the calendar dictates. If you are in any doubt seek the advice of your health visitor.

The psychology of weaning

One of the most important things to remember when you start feeding your baby is your attitude. What you think of foods – your own conditioning – is easily passed on to your baby. Many of us get a glint in our eye when we talk about cake or chocolate, so it's no wonder our children grow up thinking these foods are desirable. Likewise, if we show limited enthusiasm for, say, cauliflower or Brussels sprouts (what is it with sprouts?), when we serve them to our children they get the idea these foods aren't attractive. What you communicate to your child conditions their attitude, so say, 'Oh – delicious – try this tasty sprout,' or, 'Yummy body-building broccoli.'

Tongue-thrust reflex

Your baby has all sorts of innate survival mechanisms, which is why, for example, you can take your baby swimming as your little Thorpedo knows instinctively not to breathe under water. Well, here's another to marvel at. Babies who are too young to wean will poke their tongue out if you try to give them solids too soon. This reflex stops them from choking by clearing the throat and mouth. So if your baby is poking their tongue out at you they aren't being cheeky, they are telling you it's too soon for purées.

Avoiding allergies

A food allergy occurs when your immune system tries to protect you unnecessarily against something you've eaten. It produces antibodies it would normally generate to protect itself from infection. The body goes into overdrive producing histamine and prostaglandins, which cause swelling and a possible drop in blood pressure almost immediately after eating the offending food, resulting in some or all of the symptoms shown opposite.

How common are allergic reactions?

Food allergies and intolerances get a lot of press and there is a general belief that they are on the increase but this could be simply because we are becoming better at detecting

If your baby is at least 4 months old and shows these signs, it's time to get a hand blender

They're sitting up well without support

They're developing a 'pincer' grasp

They're starting to demand feeds more often

They've lost the tongue-thrust reflex and don't automatically push solids out of their mouth

They're a keen mealtime participant and eye up your food

They're ready and willing to chew

They used to sleep through the night but are now waking up

them. I believe that keeping food simple and, where possible, making it yourself to avoid the additives used by many manufacturers can help reduce the risk. During weaning, babies should not be given foods known to cause allergies, e.g. cow's milk, peanuts, eggs, soya and tree nuts (walnuts, pecans, etc.) and gluten-rich foods, especially wheat. Other allergenic foods include pork, fish and shellfish, oranges and citrus fruits, corn, berries, chocolate, tomatoes and food additives.

Introduce new foods as single-variety purées at or before lunchtime. Try one at a time so you can clearly identify any trouble as well as likes and dislikes. This is particularly advisable where there is a family history of food allergies.

What to do in the event of an allergic reaction

If the reaction is extreme, e.g. fainting, difficulty in breathing, swelling of the eyes, lips or tongue or there is

Allergic reactions

Breathing problems

Swelling of the lips, eyes or tongue

An increase in vomiting or posseting

Fainting

Bloating and excessive gas or diarrhoea

Skin rashes and hives

Blistering in or around the mouth

Symptoms of food intolerance

Skin rashes including eczema and hives

Bloating and excessive gas or diarrhoea

Ear infections or asthma

A runny nose and cold-like symptoms

Red, puffy eyes and eyelids, including dark circles under the eyes

Trouble sleeping, unexplained discomfort

instantaneous vomiting, call for an ambulance or take your child to the hospital immediately. Until you get help, check there is no object causing choking and loosen clothing around the neck and waist.

If you are worried about this, particularly if you or your partner have a family history of food allergies, ask your health visitor for more information on one of the many excellent courses on first aid for your infant.

Food intolerance

Food intolerance can have symptoms similar to an allergy but doesn't involve antibodies. They rarely happen immediately and are often temporary – your child can grow out of them. The delayed reaction makes it difficult to work out the cause of the problem but ongoing signs listed in the box on the left need to be investigated.

Getting started

Your baby is ready to be weaned, so it's time for a sumptuous serving of, er, baby rice. Mixed with baby's usual milk, it has a similar taste, but a slightly thicker texture. It's easy on the gut and has a low intolerance level. At this stage, milk is still the most important food. Solids are just first tastes and fillers, which should be introduced slowly over several weeks. Give your baby at least a third of their milk feed first. Then feed them some purée and finish with the rest of their milk feed. If your baby is drinking excessive amounts of milk and turning up their nose at solids, cut back on the lunchtime milk feed to stimulate the appetite.

Ready

Offer a $1/4$ teaspoon of cooked, warm baby rice on the tip of a shallow plastic spoon (metal ones can get too hot). If your baby doesn't like the taste and texture of the spoon, try putting the food on your (clean) finger and letting them suck it off. The best time of day to start is usually during the mid-morning or lunchtime feed as babies are less fussy then. This also gives you the rest of the day to keep an eye out for any reactions. After a couple of days, try a thin, runny single-ingredient vegetable puree, about the same kind of thickness as single cream. And, if this goes down a treat, repeat for a day or two, then it's time for another veg or fruit purée. Gradually make the purées a thicker consistency and try a little mixing.

Steady

If you walk down the supermarket aisle you will see an exotic array of adult-sounding recipes, supposedly suitable as first weaning foods. Compared to a simple carrot purée they may sound exciting, but remember that for the first few months of life your baby has suckled away on just one food, milk. So far from boring, the bright colours, subtle texture variation and pure taste is an adventure in itself. Learning something new will require concentration and contemplation so get ready for some impressive gurning.

Cook

Whether you intend to pan cook or steam it's important to chop the ingredients into small uniform chunks so they're all ready at the same time. At Fresh Daisy, we chop ours up into 3mm ($1/8$in) cubes. If you overcook the purée, it will lose its taste and texture. As a rule of thumb, most foods won't take more than 10 minutes. Try to use as little water as possible because vitamins such as B and C leech out into the water. If you plan to pan cook instead of steaming, the important thing is to add the fruit or vegetables to a pan of water already on a rolling boil. Where possible, add the vegetable water to the food-processor to loosen up the purée and preserve the vitamins.

Alternatively, you could steam your vegetables and fruit, which is a better way of preserving the nutrients. Remember to use the collected stock from the steamer tray as part of the purée.

If you want to microwave the food, chop into small uniform chunks, put in a microwave-friendly dish and just cover with water. Leave an air vent and cook on full power according to weight. Ensure you check and recheck the temperature of the purée as microwaves are notorious for cooking produce unevenly and microwaved food is particularly prone to hot spots. Always stir thoroughly and check the food before offering to your baby.

Feed time

Look them in the eye and be enthusiastic about their eating. It's deeeelicious food and they're a wonnnnderful eater (even if the kitchen begins to look like Jackson Pollock's been there).

So, they like food. What do you do next? Gradually increase the number of solid food feeds from one to two then three a day, slowly increasing the portions of solid food to match your baby's appetite.

Over the next couple of weeks, introduce a new vegetable or fruit every second day, so they've had a wide variety. Variety is the spice of life, and as you'll read later there's evidence to suggest that a wide spectrum of tastes will help keep a 1-year-old open-minded about food.

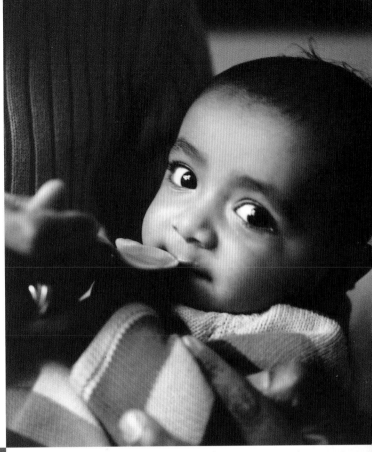

Baby rice

This is a great first weaning food. Once mixed with breast or formula milk, it seems just like thickened milk. It's bland and soft on your baby's immature digestive system and, later on, can also be an excellent food to relieve tummy upsets and diarrhoea. Rice is also gluten-free (gluten can be an allergen and is found in cereals, wheat, rye, oats and barley). You can use baby rice to thicken fruit (like pears) or vegetable purées, making them more filling.

The most convenient way to buy it is to get off-the-shelf packs from your local organic store. Simply follow the instructions on the pack.

Vegetable purées

I've tried to give you an idea of the number of servings you can expect from each recipe – the first time you try your baby on a new food you may only need a teaspoonful so I've kept the measurements pretty small so you're not swimming in purée. Once you know that your baby likes a particular variety, multiply the quantities up and freeze batches in ice-cube trays or small pots.

Sweet Potato Purée

Sweet potatoes have a nutritional soul mate in the squash family. Like the squashes, they also carry vitamin D for healthy bones and vitamin E for brassy immune systems. The orangey ones are better for your baby than the creamy colours as these contain beta-carotene or vitamin A. They also rate well on the potassium, vitamin C and fibre stakes and contain vitamin B3 or niacin, which helps to balance moods. As they're sweet with a high water content, they make an appetising first food for tiny tastebuds.
Makes 1–3 servings

1 sweet potato (approx. 100g/3½oz)

Wash and peel, then grate or finely hand chop the sweet potato to around a 3mm (⅛in) dice. The finer you chop the easier you'll find achieving a very smooth purée.

For the best results, steam for 10 minutes in an electric steamer. Alternatively in a small saucepan, bring just enough water to cover the sweet potato to a rolling boil, add the sweet potato and simmer for 10 minutes until the largest piece is soft. If you've got the oven on anyway, just give a sweet potato a scrub down, stab it all over with a fork and bake it for about 40 minutes at 150°C/300°F/gas mark 2.

Scoop out the flesh and whizz, using the chopping attachment of a hand blender, to a smooth purée, adding a little boiled water if needed to create a glossy finish.

Finally push through a fine sieve or finest-grade mouli plate.

Carrot Purée

Carrots are a perfect weaning food for beginner foodies and are an excellent source of beta-carotene, which converts in the body to vitamin A, essential for good eyesight and skin. Beta-carotene also bolsters baby's immune system and acts as an antioxidant. The darker a carrot is, the more beta-carotene it contains, so choose older carrots over baby ones. The fibre in carrots also helps your baby's gut to eliminate foods smoothly. When baby is over 6 months, add a little olive oil as the body absorbs these nutrients better with fat.

Carrots are particularly susceptible to chemicals in the soil, so even if you are still sceptical about organic at least go the extra mile here.
Makes 1–3 servings

1 medium carrot (approx. 100g/3½oz)

Wash, peel and grate or chop the carrot as per the sweet potato (left).

Steam for 10 minutes in an electric steamer. Or bring just enough water to cover the carrot to a rolling boil, add the carrot and simmer for 10 minutes until the largest piece is soft.

Whizz, using the chopping attachment of a hand blender, to a smooth purée, adding the carrot stock collected in the steamer tray to create a glossy finish.

Finally push through a fine sieve or finest-grade mouli plate.

Broccoli Purée

This 'structured' vegetable transcends the word 'superfood' and almost demands a super-dooper league of its own. This one vegetable has so much goodness. For a start, it contains vitamin K, which helps blood coagulate and strengthens bones. It's also a rich source of magnesium and – get this – one raw serving has even more calcium than a pint of milk. It's an abundant source of vitamins B and C, too. Eaten regularly, one of broccoli's nutrients, glucosinolate, can help to prevent cancer. Broccoli has antibiotic and antiviral properties so will aid your baby to stay on top of the onslaught of childhood illnesses.

Makes 1–3 servings

100g (3½oz) broccoli

Wash and, especially with organic produce, check for bugs; there will be nothing dangerous – it's just a good sign the vegetable hasn't been sprayed with chemicals.

Put the florets through the grater attachment of a food-processor or hand chop extremely finely – this will help the broccoli to cook through quickly. If you keep it as whole florets you will find you have to cook it for much longer to make the stems soft and you will lose taste and nutrients.

Steam for 8–10 minutes until the largest piece is soft. Broccoli is best steamed, but if you want to pan cook, bring 3–4 tablespoons of water to a rolling boil, then add the broccoli.

Whizz, using the chopping attachment of a hand blender, to a smooth purée, adding the broccoli stock collected in the steamer tray to create a glossy finish.

Finally push through a fine sieve or finest-grade mouli plate.

Cauliflower Purée

Cauliflower has a similar lineage to broccoli and possesses many of the same nutritional qualities as its high-flying cousin; however, like its colour, cauliflower's nutritional achievements pale slightly beside those of its exceptional relative. Cauliflower possesses strong vitamin C as well as folic acid. A word of intestinal caution, however: while cauliflower's fibres will get your baby's intestinal tract working, it can make your baby windy. Start introducing a little at a time.

Makes 1–3 servings

100g (3½oz) cauliflower

Cauliflower is delicious steamed. As with broccoli, wash and, especially with organic produce, check for bugs.

Put the florets through the grater attachment of a food-processor or hand chop extremely finely to reduce the cooking time needed.

Steam for 8–10 minutes until the largest piece is soft. Or pan cook in a saucepan with enough boiling water to cover the cauliflower. Whizz, using the chopping attachment of a hand blender, to a smooth purée, adding the cauliflower stock collected in the steamer tray to create a glossy finish.

Finally push through a fine sieve or finest-grade mouli plate.

Butternut Squash Purée

Butternut squash, or pumpkin, makes more than just a good ghoul at Halloween. As an orange-coloured veg, it – like carrot and sweet potato – is full of beta-carotene and vitamin C, an infection-busting duo. Other goodies include iron for carrying nutrients around the body and bone-building calcium and magnesium. Butternut squash also appeals to a baby's sweet palate, particularly after it's been baked in the oven, which gives it a slight caramel flavour. Mmm.

I've used butternut squash in this recipe, but red kuri is also delicious, works as well and grows in England (we need a very good summer to get a decent crop of ripe English butternut).

Makes 1–3 servings

100g (3¹/₂oz) butternut squash

Peel and remove any seeds and finely chop or grate the squash.

Steam or pan cook in 1–2 tablespoons of boiling water for 10–12 minutes until very soft.

Whizz, using the chopping attachment of a hand blender, to a smooth purée, adding the stock collected in the steamer tray or pan to create a glossy finish.

Finally push through a fine sieve or finest-grade mouli plate.

Alternatively, remove the seeds and wrap in foil (if you are doing a larger batch keep each chunk to 100g/3¹/₂oz) and bake at 150°C/300°F/gas mark 2 for around 40 minutes or until soft. Scoop the soft flesh from the skin into the chopping bowl of your blender and continue as before. If needed, add a little boiling water to blend and push through a sieve as before.

Swede Purée

You've probably heard of the swede. No, not the blond-haired, blue-eyed, rugged-looking Scandinavians, you turnip, although you're closer to the origins of the vegetable than you probably realise. The swede is our name for the root vegetable originating from Sweden, called the rotabagge, and is closely related to the cabbage and, funnily enough, the turnip. Swedes are usually purple, white or yellow in colour while the flesh should be white or a pale yellow. Like sweet potatoes and squash the vegetable is sweet to taste and makes a great stage 1 purée. Choose ones that are smooth, firm and heavy. Swedes should be kept in the fridge and should last for about two weeks.

Makes 1–3 servings

100g (3¹/₂oz) swede

Wash and peel, then grate or finely hand chop the swede into 3mm (¹/₈in) dice. The finer you chop the easier you'll find achieving a very smooth purée.

Steam for 10 minutes in an electric steamer or bring just enough water to cover the swede to a rolling boil, add the swede and simmer for 10 minutes until the largest piece is soft.

Whizz, using the chopping attachment of a hand blender, to a smooth purée, adding the stock collected in the steamer tray to create a glossy finish.

Finally push through a fine sieve or finest-grade mouli plate.

Parsnip Purée

Babies love parsnips. Like other root vegetables, these tend to be sweet. As well as iron, parsnips are rich in potassium, which is essential for the smooth functioning of muscles and nerves and also works to help the body absorb bone-growing calcium. On the vitamin front, they contain vitamins C and E as well as iron.

Makes 1–3 servings

1 parsnip (approx. 100g/3^1/$_2$oz)

Wash and peel, then grate or finely hand chop the parsnip into 3mm (^{1}/$_8$in) dice. You may need to remove the core as this can harden while cooking and then you'll struggle to get them to purée.

For best results, steam for 10 minutes in an electric steamer. Alternatively, in a small saucepan add just enough water to cover the grated parsnip, bring to the boil, add the parsnip and simmer for 10 minutes until the largest piece is soft.

Whizz, using the chopping attachment of a hand blender, to a smooth purée, adding the stock collected in the steamer tray to create a glossy finish.

Finally push through a fine sieve or finest-grade mouli plate.

If your baby finds the flavour of parsnip too strong, try mixing in a little apple or pear purée.

Pea Purée

It's a bird, it's a plane… it's super peas. Yes, these little balls are in the big nutrient league and considered an entire food in their own right. Peas have a kapow vitamin and mineral punch of vitamins A, B and C, zinc, magnesium, iron and calcium. The little pea will help your baby's immune system as well as keep their bones growing and help their brains function. Frozen peas are perfectly fine: just ensure they are used up within their freezer time and look out for supermarket varieties that are frozen on the day they are picked.

Makes 1–3 servings

100g (3^1/$_2$oz) fresh or frozen peas

For best results, steam for 10 minutes in an electric steamer. Alternatively, in a small saucepan add just enough water to cover the peas, bring to the boil, add the peas and simmer for 8 – 10 minutes until soft. Whizz, using the chopping attachment of a hand blender, to a smooth purée, adding the stock collected in the steamer tray to create a glossy finish.

Finally push through a fine sieve or finest-grade mouli plate to remove any stubborn pea skins.

Fennel Purée

Fennel may not be at the top of a list of weaning foods but you may want to consider it, especially with a baby who is suffering from colic. Weaning a baby too early increases the chances of colic and, although its causes are not completely understood, with your baby screaming the house down you'll know they've got it. Overactive bowel contractions may be the problem and this, combined with trapped wind, is a recipe for an extremely unpleasant time. Fennel makes a pale green fragrant purée and is believed to have a relaxing and calming effect.

Makes 1–3 servings

½ fennel bulb (approx. 100g/3½oz) (use the rest in a roast vegetable combo to treat yourself)

Wash, and remove the tough root bottom of the bulb and chop finely.

Steam for 5–7 minutes in an electric steamer until soft. (You can pan cook in enough boiling water to cover the fennel, but steaming will produce the best result.)

Whizz, using the chopping attachment of a hand blender, to a smooth purée, adding the stock collected in the steamer tray or pan to create a glossy finish.

Finally push through a fine sieve or finest-grade mouli plate.

Beetroot Purée

If you are fed up with all your babyfood looking pretty much the same colour then this is one to buck the trend. It's so colourful it comes with a nappy warning! Beetroot contains no fat but is a great source of fibre. Packed with iron and magnesium it is known as the vitality plant and has been used in the treatment of cancer, especially leukaemia. Strange, therefore that it has had such a bad press, but it's probably to do with the fact it has spent most of its life drowned in vinegar jars at the back of Grandma's cupboard. If there was a food Oscars this veg would definitely feel at home walking down the red carpet.

Like all root vegetables beetroot has a natural sweetness that your baby will love.

Makes 1–3 servings

1 large or 2 small fresh beetroot (approx. 100g/3½oz)

Wash, top, tail and peel the beetroot. Dice into 3mm (⅛in). cubes or use the coarse shredding attachment of a food-processor.

In a small saucepan, bring just enough water to cover the beetroot to the boil. Add the beetroot, reduce to a gentle simmer and cook for 10–12 minutes until soft. (Although beetroot can be steamed it tends to discolour the plastic of electric steamers so stick with the pan method.)

Whizz, using the chopping attachment of a hand blender, to a smooth purée, adding the stock collected in the pan to create a glossy finish.

Finally push through a fine sieve or finest-grade mouli plate.

Nappy warning! Beetroot can give your baby red pee and poo. It's not dangerous but can be a bit of a shock when you first see it.

Spinach Purée

Spinach can have quite a strong taste so choose baby rather than large leaf spinach because it's sweeter. I have kept the quantity very small as I find it's a bit of a 'love-it or hate-it' purée. Try blending with baby rice, your baby's usual milk or a tried-and-tested favourite purée to introduce for the first time.

Makes 1–2 servings

50g (2oz) fresh baby spinach leaves

Thoroughly wash the leaves, removing any tough-looking stems and tearing any larger leaves in half.

For best results, steam for 5–7 minutes in an electric steamer. Alternatively, in a small saucepan, bring to the boil just enough water to cover, add the spinach and simmer for 6–10 minutes until soft.

Whizz, using the chopping attachment of a hand blender, to a smooth purée, adding the stock collected in the steamer tray or pan to create a glossy finish.

Finally push through a fine sieve or finest-grade mouli plate to remove any stringy bits you may have missed.

Courgette Purée

The courgette (or if you're feeling posh the zucchini) is a summer squash. They are usually green or yellow and sold when they are about 13–15cm (5–6in) in size. They're a good stage 1 weaning food as they don't have a strong taste and most babies will take to them with relish. If you are bored of orange-coloured purées this makes a bright green subtle tasting purée.

Makes 1–3 servings

I small courgette (approx. 100g/3¹/₂oz)

If you can only find large courgettes the skin may be a little tough – in which case, you'll need to peel. Otherwise simply wash, top and tail then finely chop or grate.

Steam for 5–7 minutes in an electric steamer. Alternatively, in a small saucepan bring to the boil just enough water to cover, add the courgette and simmer for 6–10 minutes until soft.

Whizz, using the chopping attachment of a hand blender, to a smooth purée, adding the stock collected in the steamer tray or pan to create a glossy finish.

Finally push through a fine sieve or finest-grade mouli plate.

Green Bean Purée

These lean, mean fighting machines are bright, shiny and glossy when fresh but, like a prize fighter who has done too many rounds, they start bulging and become leafy and limp when old. Green beans are a good source of lutein, an antioxidant that is good for eye health.

Makes 1–3 servings

100g (3¹/₂oz) fresh young green beans or runner beans

Wash and finely slice the beans, removing any tough stringy strands.

For best results, steam for 6–8 minutes in an electric steamer. Alternatively, in a small saucepan bring to the boil just enough water to cover, add the beans and simmer for 8–10 minutes until soft.

Whizz, using the chopping attachment of a hand blender, to a smooth purée, adding the stock collected in the steamer tray or pan to create a glossy finish.

Finally push through a fine sieve or finest-grade mouli plate to remove any stringy bits you may have missed.

Potato Purée

I've met several parents who fully intended to make all their own babyfood, only to start with potato and then vow never to purée again either because they end up in a sticky mess or, very occasionally, because babies can be intolerant to them during the first weeks of weaning. I recommend that you hold off introducing potatoes until you and your baby are chugging away confidently with the other purées in this section.

Try potato on its own before introducing it as part of a stage 2 purée to check for any adverse reactions.

In its defence, the potato does contain the mood-leveller, vitamin B3 (niacin), which helps to create the 'happy' hormone serotonin. It is also a source of vitamin B and is high in vitamin C as well as providing energy-rich carbohydrate.

Makes 1 serving

I small potato (approx. 50g/2oz)

Wash the potato and peel unless you intend to bake it.

Pan cook the potato in just enough boiling water to cover. Or puncture holes in the potato with a fork and bake for 25 minutes at 150°C/300°F/gas mark 2.

If baked, scoop out the soft flesh, then give it a brief whizz in the chopping attachment of a hand blender. If you whizz for too long the starch is released and you'll end up with a goo resembling glue. Add a little boiled water if needed. If the cooked potato is very soft you could omit the blending stage and simply push through a fine sieve or finest-grade mouli plate.

Fruit purées

If you are struggling with any of the veg purées on the previous pages or you need to sweeten a later-stage meal the following fruit purées can be frozen and added as a natural sweetener. Just remember not to eat them all yourself.

Pear Purée

Pears are a soft, gentle first weaning food, with an extremely low likelihood of intolerance. Pears contain pectin, which helps those little bowels to start processing solids efficiently. Like most fruits, pears offer a rich source of vitamin C and iodine, which the thyroid gland craves to kick-start the metabolism and produce energy. Pears also contain small quantities of folic acid and iron.

Makes 1–3 servings

1 small ripe pear (approx. 100g/3^1/$_2$oz)

Peel and carefully core the pear, making sure you have removed all the pip husks. Chop into very small chunks or grate directly into the boiling water.

To steam, follow the Apple Purée recipe (see right).

In a small saucepan, bring 1 tablespoon of water to a rolling boil. Add the pear and simmer for 8–10 minutes until the largest piece is soft.

Whizz, using the chopping attachment of a hand blender, to a smooth purée. Finally push through a fine sieve or finest-grade mouli plate.

Apple Purée

'An apple a day...' well, you know the rest. Once introduced to apples, most babies will love them in any shape or form throughout their lives. Like pears, apples contain pectin, a soluble fibre that helps to stimulate bacteria in the gut and improves food 'elimination' (don't you just love the scientific word for poo). Apples also provide vitamin C and beta-carotene, a winning duo to bolster any fledgling immune system. In season, I love using English-grown Discovery apples for their blush pink colour and Russet, which remind me of my Grandma Daisy, who had a big tree that came into fruit to mark the beginning of autumn.

Most commercial babyfood companies use chemical treatments to prevent apples and pears from browning. This isn't necessary if the time between peeling and cooking is kept to an absolute minimum. By putting the prepared apple straight into boiling water, you'll find the purée stays pretty much the colour nature intended.

Makes 1–3 servings

^{1}/$_2$ dessert apple (approx. 100g/3^1/$_2$oz)

Peel and carefully core the apple, making sure you have removed all the pip husks. Chop the apple into very small chunks or grate directly into the steamer compartment. Steam for 8–10 minutes.

For the saucepan method follow the Pear recipe (see left).

Whizz, using the chopping attachment of a hand blender, to a smooth purée. Finally push through a fine sieve or finest-grade mouli plate.

Nectarine or Peach Purée

These fruits are close sisters. Orange-coloured varieties are full of, yet again, that immune award-winning team of beta-carotene and vitamin C, which will help your baby to ward off illnesses, particularly those who are being weaned off the immunological benefits of breastfeeding mums. When fully ripe, their flesh is deliciously sweet, which your baby will adore. Surprisingly, they are also full of iron.

Makes 1–3 servings

¹/₂ **ripe peach (approx. 100g/3¹/₂oz)**

Removing the skins of peaches (and plums) can be a messy business, resulting in lots of lost fruit, so try this way instead.

Run a sharp knife across the bottom of the fruit, place them in water on a rolling boil for about 30 seconds, remove carefully, and then dip them into iced water. Pour off the water and the skins should peel off easily.

Remove the stones and slice the fruit into a small saucepan, catching any juice as you go. Simmer, only adding a little water if necessary, until soft.

Whizz, using the chopping attachment of a hand blender, to a smooth purée. Finally push through a fine sieve or finest-grade mouli plate.

Plum Purée

Makes 1–3 servings

3–4 ripe, naturally sweet plums

Some plums have very thin skins, other are quite tough. If you can start to peel the skin (rather than it being so thin it immediately tears) follow the technique for removing the skins of peaches (see left) but plunge into very hot water rather than a rolling boil otherwise you'll end up with a squidgy mess!

Remove the stones and slice the fruit into a small saucepan, catching any juice as you go. Simmer until soft.

Whizz, using the chopping attachment of a hand blender, to a smooth purée. Finally push through a fine sieve or finest-grade mouli plate.

Mango Purée

Mangoes are one of life's treats. A juicy ripe mango not only gives your baby the immunological benefits of vitamin C and beta-carotene, but also calcium and magnesium, which are good for building strong bones and teeth. If your baby is having tummy trouble, mangoes may help, as they are highly alkaline and can balance any belly acidity issues.

I recommend cooking mango for the first few times – after that, as long as the mango is very ripe you can use the same method for Papaya Purée on page 76.

If you're new to the world of mango here's a crash course in how to tackle one. If it's ripe the skin will give slightly when you gently push on it; it will also smell fragrant. Look out for a label on the fruit saying smooth or fibrous. If you get a choice go for smooth. There is nothing wrong with the fibrous varieties, but, as the name suggests, they can leave tiny fibres in the purée, which are perfectly safe but may be a bit of a surprise.

Makes 1–3 servings

**100g (3¹/₂o ipe mango – use the rest of the fruit as a healthy
 nd de' us treat for yourself**

 es have a large flat stone through the middle. Aim to
cu either side of the stone then score the flesh with a sharp knife. You should then be able to turn the skin back in on itself so you can slice off the ready diced fruit (see photograph on page 95).

Chop the fruit up a little more over a small saucepan to catch the juice and simmer for 5 minutes until soft.

Whizz, using the chopping attachment of a hand blender, to a smooth purée. Finally push through a fine sieve or finest-grade mouli plate.

Dried Apricot or Prune Purées

Dried fruit condenses the goodness of the original fruit. Dried prunes (formerly plums) and dried apricots are an excellent source of iron, aka brain fodder. These fruits are rich in the dynamic, health-promoting duo vitamin C and beta-carotene. And, if that's not enough, they also have oodles of powerful potassium. Their natural sweetness makes them ideal for first purées. When choosing dried apricots, ensure that they're organic and are not sulphured. (Look out for those treated with sulphur dioxide or E220 as these can trigger latent asthma or allergies. Sulphur dioxide is used to keep the colour bright orange, so choose dark brown dried apricots.) Prunes are a well-known laxative, so add small quantities of these purées to other fruit purées or with baby rice and milk to begin with and assess the nappy damage.

Makes 1–3 servings

5–6 dried apricots or prunes (approx. 100g/3¹/₂oz)

Wash and finely chop the fruit, checking for any bits of stone.

Bring 2–3 tablespoons of water to a rolling boil then simmer the fruit for about 10 minutes until soft.

Whizz, using the chopping attachment of a hand blender, then push through the finest-grade mouli plate together with a little of the cooking water to make a smooth purée.

No-cook fruit purées

The following are no-cook purées. I do not recommend you start to wean your baby with these raw purées as cooked food is easier to digest. If you started weaning before 6 months I suggest that you wait until you are 4 weeks into weaning before you introduce these. Having said that, they are very easy to prepare and often adored by babies.

Banana Purée

Banana purée will probably be among your baby's – and child's – all-time favourite foods. From your point of view, bananas are perfectly portable, easy to turn into purée and they come in their own sustainable, eco-friendly packaging. They are a rich source of complex carbs (the slow-releasing type) so give your baby a sustained slow release of sugar. Like other white-coloured foods, they're a good source of potassium, which is good for nerve and muscle development. I am often asked if you can overdo the banana purée. According to oriental nutrition, bananas are described as 'damp' and can cause babies (and adults) to produce too much mucus. In other words if your baby seems rather snotty, it might be worth turning down the volume of banana purée to see if it's the culprit.

Makes 1 serving (banana purée does not freeze well – but it's really easy to make fresh each time)

½ **small banana (approx. 50g/2oz)**

Peel the banana, then whizz using the chopping attachment of a hand blender. You will need to check for lumps before feeding the purée to your baby as you cannot sieve banana purée (if you try to push banana through a sieve you'll end up with the most bizarre mix of grey liquid and revolting lumps – nice!).

Avocado Purée

Is it a fruit? Is it a vegetable? No, it's an avocado. Whatever it is, remember the avocado has incredible powers. While rich in calories, an avocado is also one of the best sources of vitamin E, which helps with wound healing, a good complexion and a robust immune system. Avocados also contain folic acid, which your baby needs as their iron sources reduce as they get older. If that wasn't enough, avocados are also full of monounsaturated fat, a good fat to give your baby energy. Oh – and they have the highest protein content of any fruit.

Makes 1 serving (avocado purée does not freeze well – but it's as easy as banana to make fresh and you can treat yourself to some of the remaining fruit in a salad)

$1/4$–$1/2$ **avocado (leave the stone in the remaining fruit to reduce browning)**

Score criss-crosses through the flesh and use a spoon to scoop out the ready chopped pieces. Whizz in the chopping attachment of a hand blender until smooth. Serve immediately as it will brown.

Papaya (Paw Paw) Purée

The papaya can grow from a seed to a 6m (20ft) fruit-producing tree in less than 18 months. The fruits are usually sold when they are about the size of a pear and have an orangey skin. Don't be too disappointed when you cut into the flesh – the fruit contains quite a few black seeds which will need to be scraped away. The flesh should be a similar colour to the skin and is a rich source of vitamins A and B.
Makes 1 serving

$1/4$–$1/2$ **papaya**

Remove the black seeds. Scoop out the flesh with a spoon and simply whizz to a smooth purée using the chopper attachment of a hand blender.

Melon Purée

'You're twisting my melons, man,' and your baby will love you for it! It's a delicious no-cook purée so introduce it into your baby's diet once they're comfortable with cooked stage 1 purées and are chomping at the bit for some variety. Galia, water or cantaloupe, they're all great for puréeing. On purchase a melon should be fragrant and firm, and a little softness is a sign it is ripe. Always keep in the fridge as they go off quickly at room temperature, but before serving leave at room temperature for 1 hour to bring out the flavour. Melons are a rich source of vitamins A, C and potassium but not good for freezing as they have a high water count.

Makes 1 serving (not suitable for freezing)

$1/8$ **medium melon**

Remove any seeds. Cut the flesh from the skin and simply whizz to a smooth purée using the chopper attachment of a hand blender.

First spoonfuls

Choose the late morning/early lunch feed to introduce new foods when you and your baby feel more ready for new experiences. The volume of breast or formula milk needed depends on age and weight, so vary accordingly.

	Wake-up/ Breakfast	Late morning/Lunch	Mid-afternoon	Dinner	Bedtime
Days 1–2	Breast milk or formula milk (about 220ml/ 8fl oz)	Breast milk or formula milk (about 220ml/ 8fl oz) 1–2 teaspoons baby rice made with baby's usual milk	Breast milk or formula milk (about 180ml/ 6fl oz)	Breast milk or formula milk (about 220ml/ 8fl oz)	Breast milk or formula milk (about 180ml/ 6fl oz)

First tastes

Introduce a purée over two consecutive days. If your baby prefers, mix the purée with a little baby rice.

	Wake-up/ Breakfast	Late morning/Lunch	Mid-afternoon	Dinner	Bedtime
Days 3–8	Breast milk or formula milk (about 220ml/ 8 fl oz)	Breast milk or formula milk (about 220ml/ 8fl oz) 1–2 teaspoons of: Days 3 & 4 **Sweet Potato Purée** (p60) Days 5 & 6 **Carrot Purée** (p60) Days 7 & 8 **Pear or Apple Purée** (p70)	Breast milk or formula milk (about 180ml/ 6fl oz)	Breast milk or formula milk (about 220ml/ 8fl oz)	Breast milk or formula milk (about 100ml/ 3½fl oz)

Developing tastes

Remember all babies differ in preferences and appetites, so vary the purées and quantities to suit your baby. Follow this meal planner until you and your baby are comfortable with it, then move on to stage 2. Do not begin stage 2 until your baby is 6 months old. If your baby was an early weaner, repeat stage 1 until your child reaches 6 months.

	Wake-up/ Breakfast	Late morning/ Lunch	Mid-afternoon	Dinner	Bedtime
Weeks 2–4	Breast milk or formula milk (about 220ml/ 8 fl oz) Stage 1 **fruit purées** (see p70–76)	Breast milk or formula milk (about 220ml/ 8 fl oz) Stage 1 **vegetable purées** (see p60–69)	Breast milk or formula milk (about 180ml/ 6fl oz)	Breast milk or formula milk (about 200ml/ 7fl oz) Optional: baby rice with your baby's favourite purée	Breast milk or formula milk (about 100ml/ 3½fl oz)

Stage two:
Textures and new tastes

Your child has become an eating machine and their first teeth are beginning to show. This section introduces new tastes and textures into their diet.

The second stage

Your baby's mouth has become a magnet – everything goes straight from their hand to their mouth. It's all part of their oral investigation of the expanding horizon around them. Your baby's muscular and skeletal development means that they now sit up confidently and are learning to reach, grasp, grab, pull, pinch and hold. What's more, your baby's vision is also sharpening to an adult depth and they want to touch what they see. It's all exciting stuff and it means that it's high time to move on to the next stage of weaning, but do not begin this stage until your baby is 6 months old.

You'll both be feeling pretty comfortable with stage 1 purées, so it's time to get that little inquisitive mouth working harder. Learning to take 'bits' into the mouth and knowing how to swallow them is a new skill which requires your baby to start fine-tuning some tongue control – as well as learning to eat this stage is also thought to be an important step in learning to speak.

What to expect

Expect your stage 2 weaner to look at you with a confused face and then spit out the new textured purées. Don't be alarmed; although some babies take to texture like a duck to water, many are sceptical – it just requires more patience than easy-to-swallow, smooth purées. Choose the early feeds to introduce new textures as you did for new tastes – both you and your baby will feel fresher for a lesson in texture. Try not to feel pressured and if your baby is reluctant, go back to smooth purées for a day or two before trying again. It is an important step forward and worth persisting with.

First textures

Texture doesn't mean lumps. The purées should contain bits no bigger than 3mm ($^1/_8$in), be soft enough to be squashed between your tongue and the roof of your mouth and be swallowed without chewing. It's almost like 'drinking' the purée in two swallows – the first for the wetter part of the purée, the second to finish off the squidgy bits. Taste it yourself first: if you have to chew, the lumps are too big. Also, during stage 2 you will begin to recognise the recipes as the kind of food you would eat, admittedly through a straw, but it's a start.

Your trainee muncher is well on the way to solids so confirm their new status in life by placing them at the top of the culinary world in a high chair.

Milk

Remember breast or formula milk is still your baby's primary food source and around 500–600ml (18fl oz– 1 pint) should be consumed every day including the milk used in cooking. Fresh cow's milk is a no-no for the first 12 months – which can cause some confusion as dairy products are often promoted as suitable for babies less than 1 year old. This is because the method used to make yogurts, fromage frais, hard cheeses and the like makes them easier to digest, therefore safer for your baby than cow's milk. However, it is during stage 3 that these products really start to feature.

What's new in stage 2

Texture: purées, with bits in

Cereals: including oat-based porridge, millet and quinoa grain

Iron-rich foods become essential

Protein-rich foods: including lentils, tofu, poultry, meat and fish

Eggs, but make sure they are well cooked (avoid if there is a family history of allergies)

Iron man

Their fledgling teeth and growing bones will need a significant nutrient boost to help sustain their development, so having the full complement of vitamins and minerals, iron and proteins increases in importance.

In particular this stage sees the rising importance of iron and the introduction of proteins. Having been on solid foods for a month your baby is now more active and going through an incredible rate of growth so you will have to increase the number of feeds and the amount they are eating. Your baby is born with iron reserves which in conjunction with breast milk or formula are sufficient up to 6 months. After that time iron is also needed from the diet.

Getting enough iron into your baby's system enables blood to carry oxygen around the body, feeding brain development. A lack of iron can mean that your child lacks

energy and, in the worst-case scenario, may develop anaemia. This stage therefore sees plenty of iron-rich fruits and vegetables (apricots, peaches, raisins, prunes, bananas, avocados, spinach and broccoli) and also marks the introduction of poultry and fish. Towards the end of stage 2 there is a recipe for your baby's first encounter with egg – the yolk is another iron-rich food.

It's also worth noting that vitamin C helps the absorption of iron so meals combining vitamin C and iron-rich ingredients are a winner, as is a serving of fruit purée as a dessert after an iron-rich main.

Vegetarian babies and iron

Parents wanting to bring up their child on a vegetarian diet should be aware there are two types of iron: non-haem and haem. Non-haem iron, found in vegetables, fruits, lentils, dried beans and grain, is less readily absorbed by the body than the haem iron in rich animal products, so in order to ensure that your baby gets the necessary levels seek meal-planning advice from the Vegetarian Society, who have excellent info packs on weaning.

Protein pack

It's also time to introduce proteins, one of the body's essential building blocks. Start with simple fruit and vegetable sources such as lentil, quinoa or tofu. Once your baby is doing well with these, you can then introduce recipes with good-quality organic chicken and fish.

You can substitute chicken for organic lean beef or lamb mince – both are rich in iron and protein – but avoid pork, including ham and bacon, because it's too high in salt and saturated fat.

Organic fish

Buying organic salmon and trout should be pretty easy but finding organic white fish will prove difficult. To be certified organic, fish has to be farmed to ensure it is fed a purely organic diet – instead look for high-quality wild, white fish from sustainable stocks.

Teething

Ouch! Just as your baby is settling to a good night's sleep they start the painful business of teething. If you've ever had a toothache, you'll know how it hurts, so don't be surprised to find them stuffing anything into their mouths to alleviate the pain. Your baby may become irritable and eat erratically. Pressing hard, cool objects against their swollen gums helps them to cut their teeth. Their pearly white teeth should start popping up from 6 months onwards and about 4 to 8 teeth are usually smiling at you by the age of 12 months.

The enamel on these newly erupting teeth is immature and vulnerable. They need careful looking after because they act as 'holders' and guide in the adult teeth. Looking after your baby's teeth – and creating good food habits – can save a lifetime of dental work.

Tooth decay

Decay is caused by an acid in dental plaque, produced by bacteria feeding on the sugars we eat or drink. The acid attacks the hard enamel, producing holes and breaking down the softer dentine. One of the most common ways for teeth to be exposed to danger is from a baby's bottle.

Obvious drinks to watch out for are milk, formula and fruit juice. The sugars in these liquids sit on infants' teeth and gums, feeding the bacteria that cause plaque.

Never allow your child to fall asleep with a bottle in their mouth. Tooth decay is also associated with children whose pacifiers are frequently dipped in honey, sugar or syrup. The sweet fluids left in the mouth increase the chances of cavities developing while the infant is sleeping. Be careful also not to give your baby a sweet drink just before nap time as saliva production slows down during sleep, allowing the sugars to have their very own mouth party.

The more sugar your baby eats, the more likely it is that their teeth will suffer damage. Eating other foods at the same time as sugar or sugary foods dilutes the acid generated and reduces the harmful effects of sugar, so keep sugary foods for mealtimes.

Teething-friendly foods

Freshly grated fruits or soft mushy fruits like mango or banana

Textured purées

For babies who are confident with finger foods, try:

Steamed carrot batons or vegetable sticks with a dip

Chilled cucumber, carrot or fruit sticks

Mini breadsticks, rice cakes or low-sugar rusks

Make sure you brush your baby's teeth thoroughly twice a day. Use a bespoke baby toothbrush with soft fibres or in times of very painful teething a clean, soft cloth wrapped around your finger. Just use a pea-sized blob of toothpaste. Interestingly, it's the use of fluoride as much as brushing that helps to prevent decay. Brushing last thing at night is very important and you should do it for your child until they are 6 or 7 as most small people don't have the manual dexterity to brush properly. Studies show that children who brush more than once a day show the least decay.

If you want to minimise the amount of sugar in your baby's diet, remember that milk is high in lactose, so try dropping the night feeds. At night, the mouth produces less saliva than usual, which means that a sugary coating will cling to the teeth. If your baby insists on drinking at night, try a bottle of cooled boiled water instead.

Breakfast ideas

Full English and a cup of tea? Not quite at this age but the principle is the same. Walk past any traditional café at 7 in the morning and it'll be crammed with burly blokes in overalls readying themselves for a busy day of standing around, looking at problems and saying, 'That'll cost you'! The point being a good, healthy feed in the morning will set your child up for the day and hopefully get them into a healthy routine for the rest of their life.

Banana and Prune Purée

Makes 1 serving (not suitable for freezing)

25g (1oz) prunes (or dried apricots, not treated with sulphur)

½ banana

Cut the prunes into very small pieces. Bring to the boil just enough water to cover, add the prunes and simmer until soft.

Whizz with a hand blender together with the banana and serve as is, with baby's usual milk or, for the older child, swirled through natural yogurt.

Millet and Fruits

Makes 1 serving

40g (1½oz) seasonal fruit or 2–3 frozen cubes of fruit purée

25g (1oz) millet flakes

Wash, peel and chop the fruit (this recipe works very well with apples, peaches and even dried fruits).

In a saucepan, add enough water to cover the fruit, bring to the boil, add the fruit and simmer until soft. Alternatively, defrost the cubes.

Sprinkle in the millet flakes, stirring continuously as it will thicken quickly. Add some of your baby's usual milk if the mixture becomes too thick.

Beginner's Porridge

Oats are not gluten-free, although are thought to have a different type of gluten from wheat, and are therefore not supposed to cause the same digestive problems in gluten-intolerant babies.

Makes 1 serving (not suitable for freezing if using banana)

100ml (3½fl oz) of your baby's usual milk
15g (¾oz) rolled oats

2–4 frozen cubes of your baby's favourite fruit purée or ½ small banana, mashed

Heat the baby's milk in a saucepan, stirring in the oats. Bring to the boil then reduce to a simmer, stirring occasionally until it thickens, then melt in the fruit cubes or add the mashed banana.

Whizz briefly with a hand blender if the texture is still a little too coarse for the weaning stage.

Allow to cool and serve.

No-gluten Muesli

Most breakfast cereals are wheat based and therefore high in gluten and recently there has been a trend towards reducing or even excluding gluten in the first year. This recipe uses a couple of unusual grains which are gluten-free as well as nutritionally packed with goodness. Quinoa is particularly useful as it provides essential amino acids normally only found in meat and dairy, as well as iron and calcium (so is particularly worth noting for parents bringing up their babies on a vegetarian diet). The added fruit helps the absorption of the minerals and brings vitamins C and D along to the breakfast party, making it a great way to start the day for grown-ups as well as babies.

Makes 1–3 servings

15g (³⁄₄oz) quinoa grain
4 dried apricots (check they are not treated with sulphur) or 50g (2oz) sultanas

¹⁄₂ dessert apple
15g (³⁄₄oz) millet flakes
Pinch of cinnamon (optional)

Cover the quinoa with water, bring to the boil then simmer for 10 minutes.

Chop the apricots, then peel the apple and chop. Add the apricots and apple to the quinoa and simmer for a further 10 minutes until the grains are soft (they will go transparent). Add more water as needed. Stir in the millet flakes and cinnamon, if using, and gently cook for a further 3–5 minutes.

Whizz with a hand blender to break down the grains, adding more boiling water to give the purée a glossy shine.

Serve on its own, mix in your baby's usual milk or mashed banana or, for the older child, swirl with yogurt.

Freeze the remainder, but note that a little more water or your baby's usual milk may be needed when defrosting.

Veggie and fruit combos

Your baby should be chomping at the bit by now, so it's time to up the ante on the texture. They will be comfortable with various individual fruits and veg in stage 1, so similarly at this stage if there is a new fruit or veg on the menu, combine it with other ingredients you know they like and introduce it into their diet at lunchtime so you can monitor any reactions. You can also start introducing a range of flavours in slightly more complicated recipes.

I suggest starting with Apple and Pear (see page 96) and Carrot and Sweet Potato (see below) as they are usually a safe bet for a child because the taste is quite sweet.

Carrot and Sweet Potato Purée

Sweet potatoes are easier to digest than standard potatoes and like carrots have a natural sweetness making both great stage 1 purées. This combo is our number one savoury tip for introducing first textures – it's almost a stage 1.

The aim is to introduce texture gradually to get your baby used to dealing with bits.

Makes 1–3 servings

75g (3oz) carrot
75g (3oz) sweet potato

Chopped fresh coriander to add taste for the more confident weaner (optional)

Wash, then peel the carrots and sweet potato. Finely dice in a food processor or chop into approx 3mm (1/8in) cubes.

Steam for 10–15 minutes or until the sweet potato is completely soft. The carrot should hold its shape but be easily squashed between your fingers or by your tongue on the roof of your mouth. Alternatively bring to the boil just enough water to cover the vegetables, add the vegetables and simmer for 15 minutes. For the more confident weaner, add the coriander for the last 5 minutes of cooking.

Whizz with a hand blender or push through a sieve or mouli adding the collected stock from the steamer tray or the water used to boil the veg to make a glossy purée.

Tip See page 39 for how to turn this into a delicious soup for adults.

Seasonal Root Vegetable Purée

Turnips, swedes and parsnips may not play a large part in your diet but don't overlook them for your baby. Take a taste yourself and you may be pleasantly surprised, because root vegetables are naturally sweet. However, they are particularly susceptible to pesticides so search out organic, seasonal, locally grown treats whenever you can.

Makes 1–2 servings

50g (2oz) carrot or parsnip
50g (2oz) sweet potato or potato

50g (2oz) swede or turnip or beetroot*

Wash and peel the vegetables (removing the tough/stringy cores if needed).

Finely chop in a food-processor to make 3mm (1/8in) dice or use a cheese grater to make fine strips. Steam for 10 minutes, or bring to the boil just enough water to cover the vegetables, add the vegetables and cook until soft enough to squeeze between your fingers.

Whizz with a hand blender or push through a sieve or mouli (if hand blending, potato will go sticky and glue-like if you overblend – stick to short blasts and stir to check for lumps).

Nappy warning! See the beetroot warning on page 66.

Potato, Parsnip and Pear Purée

This may seem an odd combination and has become our company's version of Marmite. Some people love it, others just can't get their heads round the taste. Whether it's a preconceived idea of fruit and vegetable not going together, I don't know, but just think of pineapples on a savoury pizza and you start to understand where I'm heading with this. It's a nice one if your baby is struggling with vegetables as the parsnips have a natural sweetness and, combined with the potatoes, give a great texture. Don't blitz it for too long as the starch will come out of the potatoes and you'll end up with a gluey mess. This recipe won a 'Commended' at the Organic Food Awards.

Makes 1–3 servings

50g (2oz) potato
50g (2oz) parsnip

50g (2oz) ripe pear

Wash, peel and chop the vegetables to 3mm ($1/8$in) cubes – you may need to remove the hard core from the parsnip.

Next bring the potato to a rolling boil in just enough water to cover, then add the parsnips and simmer both for about 6 minutes until they begin to soften.

Finally add the pear, return to a boil and simmer for a further 4–5 minutes until all the cubes are soft.

If needed, whizz with a hand blender or push through a sieve or mouli.

Broccoli, Cauliflower and Potato Purée

This recipe always attracts a lot of questions, especially on how to cook the broccoli. Broccoli is a tricky one: undercook and it can be too crunchy, overcook and it becomes waterlogged, loses its texture, goes greyish and smells unpleasant. Cooked just right, however, broccoli has a fragrant aroma, a lovely texture and is a lush green colour. This is the real tester for a commercial babyfood company – people who use processed babyfood can't get over how our product actually smells of broccoli!

A waterlogged purée in this recipe usually means that the florets are too large and need to be cooked for too long to reach the required texture. The trick? Chop to a uniform 3mm ($1/8$in) in a food-processor, then cook in water already on a rolling boil or in a steamer at temperature.

Makes 1–3 servings

60g (2½oz) potato
50g (2oz) broccoli

50g (2oz) cauliflower

Wash and peel the potato. Rinse the broccoli and cauliflower, checking for any organic bugs.

Chop the potato, broccoli and cauliflower using the grater blade of a food-processor into 3mm ($1/8$in) dice or finely hand chop.

Tip the mix into a pan containing 4–5 tablespoons of boiling water and cook for 8–10 minutes until the largest piece is soft. Or steam in an electric steamer.

If needed, whizz with a hand blender or push through a sieve or mouli.

Pea and Bean Purée

Both vegetables are a great source of protein, fibre and iron and as they have soft textures they whizz up into a wonderful purée. Mushy peas may have a bad press but if they are made with fresh or frozen, rather than tinned peas, they have a wonderfully vibrant colour and a really fresh taste.
Makes 1–3 servings

60g (2¹/₂oz) peas, mangetout or sugar snap peas (fresh or frozen)

60g (2¹/₂oz) runner, green or French beans

Rinse the peas, top and tail the mangetout or sugar snap peas, if using. Rinse, top, tail and remove any tough, stringy bits from the beans.

Steam or simmer for 8–10 minutes . Push through a mouli to remove any hard pea husks, adding a little of the steamer stock or cooking water to produce a glossy-textured purée.

Sweet Red Pepper, Carrot and Cauliflower Purée

This combo makes an impressively colourful purée – you can replace the red pepper with yellow, orange or even green peppers, but note green pepper is not as sweet.
Makes 1–2 servings

60g (2¹/₂oz) carrot
50g (2oz) cauliflower

40g (1¹/₂oz) red pepper

Wash, peel and grate the carrot. For best results, steam the carrot while you prepare the cauliflower and red pepper.

Wash the cauliflower and pepper, removing the seeds and the white pith. Finely hand chop or put through the coarsest grater attachment of a food-processor.

Add to the carrot and continue to steam for a further 6–8 minutes until the largest piece is tender. Blend to a purée.

Spinach and Sweet Potato Purée

Spinach has less ready-to-use iron than dried apricots and tuna but is brimming with calcium, magnesium, potassium and folic acid. Its real strength is vitamin A, particularly lutein, which helps eyesight. Spinach has a slightly bitter taste, which is why I suggest using sweeter baby spinach and matching it with a vegetable that is naturally sweet.
Makes 1–2 servings

75g (3oz) sweet potato

60g (2¹/₂oz) fresh baby spinach

Wash, peel and grate or chop the sweet potato. Wash the spinach, checking over for any bugs.

Although this can be cooked in a saucepan, steaming is better as the nutrients in spinach are easily destroyed by overcooking. For best results, steam the sweet potato for 5 minutes then add the spinach leaves and cook together for 3–5 minutes, until the largest pieces of sweet potato can be squished between your finger and thumb.

Whizz with a little of the steamer stock, in a hand blender.

Leek, Carrot and Potato Mash

Makes 1–2 servings

50g (2oz) carrot
60g (2¹/₂oz) potato, (or sweet potato)

25g (1oz) leek
1 tablespoon baby's usual milk

Wash, peel and finely chop (to 3mm/¹/₈in) cubes) the carrot and potato. Bring 2 tablespoons of water to a boil, add the carrot and potato and simmer for 5 minutes.

Rinse the leek, cut lengthways then crossways into dice and add to the potato and carrot together with the milk. Simmer for a further 5 minutes until the largest piece is tender, then mash adding more baby's milk as needed.

Peach, Plum and Vanilla Purée

A real summer treat. The purée has a wonderfully rich colour and a sweet and sour taste which will make your baby pucker up as the sharpness of the plums kicks in. Get the camera out! Their face will be a treat, but after the initial surprise, they'll be reaching out for the spoon to get more. The vanilla adds another dimension and this combination really gets the whole of the mouth's taste buds working. Older children and adults love this either drizzled over ice cream or on its own. This recipe picked up a 'Highly Commended' at the Organic Food Awards.

Makes 2–3 servings

2 small or 1 large peach	1 vanilla pod, 1–2cm (1/2–1in)
2–3 plums	length

Removing the skins of peaches and plums can be a messy business ending up with lots of lost fruit, so try running a sharp knife across the bottom of each fruit, place in water on a rolling boil for about 30 seconds, remove carefully, then dip them into iced water. Pour off the water and the skins should peel off easily.

Remove the stones and slice the fruit into a small saucepan, catching any juice as you go.

Cut the vanilla pod, down the middle, on a chopping board. Bring the tip of the knife down the inside of the pod and the sticky black vanilla seeds will collect on the knife. Scrape the residue in with the peaches and plums.

Simmer, only adding a little water if necessary, until soft. Whizz in a blender to a slightly textured purée. The slight flecking through the mix is the vanilla.

Tip For a grown-up treat, pour the mix into a plastic container and freeze for 30 minutes. Remove and fluff up with a fork, freeze again and repeat until it forms a granita. Serve in a posh glass topped with a sprig of mint.

Plum and Melon Purée

Makes 1 serving (not suitable for freezing, but is easy to make)

60g (2 1/2 oz) plum purée (see page 73) or 2–3 frozen cubes	60g (2 1/2 oz) melon (honeydew or galia)

Defrost the plum purée, if necessary, then pour into the chopping bowl attachment of a hand blender.

Remove any seeds from the melon, then scoop the melon flesh from the skin and add to the blender bowl. Whizz for a few seconds to make a slightly textured purée.

This is also delicious made with fresh, ripe peaches or nectarines instead of plums.

Nectarine and Dried Apricot Purée

Iron-rich and delicious.
Makes 1 serving

3–4 dried apricots (stoned and   1 ripe nectarine
  not treated with sulphur)

Wash the apricots and chop, removing any bits of the stone or stalk. Place in a small pan with 2 tablespoons of boiling water and simmer until soft and plump, about 7–9 minutes. If you are planning to make a large batch I'd recommend washing then soaking the apricots overnight as this softens the dried fruit and reduces the cooking time.

  Wash and peel the nectarine if the skin is tough. Cut in half to remove the stone, slice the fruit and add to the apricot. Continue to cook for a further 2–3 minutes.

  Remove any larger bits of nectarine skin then whizz with a hand blender.

Tip Treat yourself and any older kids to some of this purée swirled with yogurt or on ice cream.

Dried Fruit Compote

Dried fruit is handy to have in the cupboard, especially when time is not on your side. A good mix of prunes, dried apricots, currants, dried apple, sultanas and raisins will provide calcium, iron and vitamins A, B2 and B6.
Makes 1 serving

75g (3oz) mixed dried fruit   – check they have not been
  (currants, prunes apple,   treated with sulphur)
  sultanas and raisins, apricots

If you have the time or inclination soak the dried fruit mix overnight to soften, then simply rinse and cover with 100–150ml (3½fl oz –¼ pint) boiling water. Cover and allow to cool, then refrigerate overnight.

  Or rinse then chop the dried fruit mix into 3mm (⅛in) dice – you can do this by hand or in a food-processor. Bring 100ml (3½fl oz) water to the boil in a small saucepan. Add the dried fruit to the water and reduce to a simmer. Cover and simmer for about 20 minutes, adding a little more water as needed, until the largest piece is soft.

  For added creaminess, add a couple of tablespoons of your baby's usual milk instead of the extra water.

  If needed, whizz with the blender.

Pear, Raisin and Sultana Purée

In the great tradition of the American dream, the raisin (although there are records of sun-dried grapes dating back to 1500 BC) has been written into American folklore by a supreme piece of opportunism. After a heatwave in San Francisco in 1873, the grapes left shrivelled and withered were relabelled by a grocer as a 'Peruvian Delicacy' and flew off the shelf.

Makes 1 serving

1 ripe pear
1 dessertspoon raisins and
  sultanas

Pinch of cinnamon (optional)

Wash and peel the pear. Cut in quarters, cut out the core and finely chop.

Bring a couple of teaspoons of water to the boil, add the pear and reduce to a simmer. If the pear is not particularly juicy you will need to add a little extra water.

Halve or quarter the raisins and sultanas and stir into the pear with the cinnamon, if using. Cover and simmer for 8–10 minutes.

Whizz with a hand blender before serving.

Strawberry and Banana Purée

If your child is hungry and making a racket it's time to serve up that great Wimbledon institution: strawberries (without the cream and champagne). Your child will love these sweet little summer fruits (see below for other suggested fruits) which are rich in vitamin C and beta-carotene.

These innocent little fruits (and berries and kiwis) come with a warning because they can cause irritation in children with sensitive skin or eczema. Mixing it with banana is a good idea because you can blend in a half or a quarter of a strawberry. Watch out for soreness around the mouth or blistering.

Makes 1 serving

1 small banana

50g (2oz) strawberries or kiwi
  (or other berries, including
  blueberries, raspberries or
  blackberries)

Simply whizz the peeled banana with the washed berries until smooth or slightly textured.

If preparing for older children, simply mash together with a fork.

This recipe is a great dip for older children (see page 128) and also a fantastic substitute for sugary jams and spreads.

Mango with Blackberry Ripple

Part of learning to enjoy eating is the visual experience as well as the taste. These two purées have strong contrasting colours and make a feast for the eyes as well as the tummy.
Makes 1–3 servings

½ **small ripe mango (if there is a choice select smooth rather than fibrous flesh)**

50g (2oz) **fresh blackberries**

Cut the mango in half lengthways either side of the large stone. Score the inside of the flesh and turn the skin back on itself (see photograph below). Using a small sharp knife slice the cubes off the skin. (If the mango is not ripe enough this may not work – in which case you'll have to peel and slice the fruit off the stone.)

Either steam the mango flesh or simmer in a little boiling water (as little as possible) until very soft. Whizz in the chopping bowl of a hand blender, keeping a little texture.

Wash the blackberries and simmer in ½ tablespoon of water for 8 minutes. Push the fruit through a fine sieve with the back of a metal spoon or mouli through the finest grade to remove the pips.

Drop a few spoonfuls into a serving of mango purée and swirl round with a spoon. This can be frozen as separate ice cubes or half fill with the mango purée and top up with the blackberry purée to make two-tone blocks.

Apple and Mango Purée

This is simply delicious, and being honest there are times when I'll venture off to the freezer and defrost some to eat with vanilla ice cream. This is a great, easy weaner for your baby, with a natural sweetness they will love. Apples have a grainy texture, while the mangoes are more stringy but together they are a perfect combo for a child who is being launched into the world of texture. Mangoes are rich in vitamin C and beta-carotene and also contain calcium and magnesium which help to build strong bones and teeth. Mangoes are highly alkaline so will help balance out any acidity in your baby's stomach.

Makes 1 serving

1 small dessert apple (approx 100g/3½oz)	40g (1½oz) mango

Core and peel the apple, making sure you remove all the pips and husks.

Bring 1 tablespoon of water to the boil, then grate the apple into the boiling water – this will keep browning to a minimum.

Finely slice the mango into the apple – if the mango is very ripe hold it over the pan so you capture all the juice. Or very briefly whizz in the bowl chopper of a hand blender and pour the juicy mix into the pan. Simmer for 6–8 minutes until the apple is soft, then push through a mouli or give a short sharp whizz with the blender.

Apple and Pear Purée

Like the Carrot and Sweet Potato Purée, this is a simple combination of purées that you know your child is already comfortable with. I recommend having a stock of this in the freezer as it is brilliant for filling a gap if your baby is screaming the house down.

Makes 1 serving

1 medium dessert apple	1 medium ripe pear

If you have an apple corer, run it down the middle of the apple. Quarter the pear and remove the core. Make sure you remove all the pips, pith and the stalk. Then peel the apple and pear and dice into 3mm (⅛in) squares.

Steam or pan cook with just a couple of teaspoons of boiling water for 10 minutes (you'll only need more if the pear is not very juicy) then push through a mouli or give a short sharp whizz with a hand blender.

Avoid making the purée too smooth – this non-challenging purée is great for a first lesson in texture.

Weeks 4–6: First Textures

Timings and recipes are a rough guide, but this meal planner begins to shape into a more grown-up pattern of mealtimes. The volume of breast or formula milk needed depends on age and weight, so vary accordingly.

   If your baby is struggling to cope with these textures, try puréeing a little more or go back to very smooth for two days then try again. Introduce new tastes and textures in the morning or at lunchtime.

   Remember to include a drink of water with mealtimes.

	Wake-up	Breakfast	Lunch	Mid-afternoon	Dinner	Supper	Bedtime (optional)
Day 1	Breast milk or formula milk (about 220ml/ 8fl oz)	Apple and Pear Purée (see p96)	Carrot and Sweet Potato Purée (see p86)	Breast milk or formula milk (about 180ml/ 6fl oz)	Butternut Squash Purée (see p64)	Breast milk or formula milk (about 200ml/ 7fl oz)	Breast milk or formula milk (about 50ml/ 2fl oz)*
Day 2	Breast milk or formula milk (about 220ml/ 8fl oz)	Apple and Mango Purée (see p96)	Seasonal Root Vegetable Purée (see p86)	Breast milk or formula milk (about 180ml/ 6fl oz)	Avocado Purée (see p76)	Breast milk or formula milk (about 200ml/ 7fl oz)	Breast milk or formula milk (about 50ml/ 2fl oz)*
Day 3	Breast milk or formula milk (about 220ml/ 8fl oz)	Apple and Pear Purée (see p96)	Broccoli, Cauliflower and Potato Purée (see p87)	Breast milk or formula milk (about 180ml/ 6fl oz)	Mashed Banana (see p75)	Breast milk or formula milk (about 200ml/ 7fl oz)	Breast milk or formula milk (about 50ml/ 2fl oz)*
Day 4	Breast milk or formula milk (about 220ml/ 8fl oz)	Nectarine and Dried Apricot Purée (see p92)	Potato, Parsnip and Pear Purée (see p87)	Breast milk or formula milk (about 180ml/ 6fl oz)	Carrot Purée (see p60)	Breast milk or formula milk (about 200ml/ 7fl oz)	Breast milk or formula milk (about 50ml/ 2fl oz)*
Day 5	Breast milk or formula milk (about 220ml/ 8fl oz)	Apple and Mango Purée (see p96)	Squash and Red Lentil Purée (see p99)	Breast milk or formula milk (about 180ml/ 6fl oz)	Carrot and Sweet Potato Purée (see p86)	Breast milk or formula milk (about 200ml/ 7fl oz)	Breast milk or formula milk (about 50ml/ 2fl oz)*
Day 6	Breast milk or formula milk (about 220ml/ 8fl oz)	Pear, Raisin and Sultana Purée (see p93)	Minty Pea and Potato Purée (see p103)	Breast milk or formula milk (about 180ml/ 6fl oz)	Seasonal Root Vegetable Purée (see p86)	Breast milk or formula milk (about 200ml/ 7fl oz)	Breast milk or formula milk (about 50ml/ 2fl oz)*
Day 7	Breast milk or formula milk (about 220ml/ 8fl oz)	No-gluten Muesli (see p85)	Squash and Red Lentil Purée (see p99)	Breast milk or formula milk (about 180ml/ 6fl oz)	Mashed Banana (see p75)	Breast milk or formula milk (about 200ml/ 7fl oz)	Breast milk or formula milk (about 50ml/ 2fl oz)*

* Optional, although many babies find it a comforting part of their bedtime routine

Introducing proteins

Our body needs 22 amino acids to run efficiently but only produces 13, so the way to get them is to introduce protein into the diet. Here are some great veggie meals packed full of protein followed by some fish and meat options.

Squash and Red Lentil Purée

You might expect one of the desserts to be my favourite but this savoury treat gets my lips smacking and stomach rumbling. With a homely, comforting aroma and heart-warming taste it's won Organic Food Awards two years running including 'Overall Winner of the Babyfood' category. Not only is this recipe simple to make, lentils introduce building block proteins into your baby's diet.

Makes 1–2 servings

25g (1oz) dried red lentils

75g (3oz) squash (butternut squash or red kuri are best)

Rinse the lentils in a sieve with cold water. In a clean saucepan add enough cold water to cover the lentils and bring gently to the boil. Add more water as needed. Cut the squash in half and scoop out the seeds. Lay the squash flat side down on a clean chopping board and remove the skin with a potato peeler. Either chop to a fine dice or whizz though a food-processor to 3mm ($1/8$in) dice.

Add the squash to the lentils and bring to a rolling boil, then reduce to a simmer for a further 10 minutes, stirring occasionally, until the lentils and squash are soft enough to be squashed between your tongue and the roof of your mouth. The lentils will change from opaque to semi clear.

Push through a mouli or a metal sieve or quickly whizz with a hand blender.

Tip Make up a large batch and use some for a comforting grown-up soup – simply add some stock (see page 118) and a little seasoning.

Dhal

Makes 1–2 servings

25g (1oz) dried red lentils
125ml (4fl oz) water
15g (¾oz) onion or leek

½ teaspoon fresh parsley
Pinch of ground cumin
Pinch of ground cinnamon

Rinse the lentils thoroughly. In a saucepan, add enough water to cover the lentils and simmer for 15 minutes.

Finely chop the onion and parsley, and stir into the lentil mix with the cumin and cinnamon. Simmer for a further 10 minutes, adding more water as needed, until the lentils are soft enough to be squashed between your finger and thumb.

If the onion is chopped small enough and the mix has been sufficiently cooked, further blending won't be needed; simply cool and serve or freeze.

Kiwi, Prune and Tofu Purée

Furry brown kiwis are actually a berry, which is why kiwis are nutritionally different and superior to other fruits. Looks, you see, just like Clark Kent, are deceiving. By day the kiwi looks like a boring soul in a frumpy brown suit but come dinner time, it's changed into a green superfood. Just one serving of kiwi fruit will give you 10 per cent of your recommended daily allowance for vitamin E and your full day's vitamin C quota. A kiwi also contains more vitamin C than an orange and more potassium than a banana. The tiny black seeds are also a rich source of essential fatty acid which is rarely found outside seeds, oils and nuts. Unlike the New Zealand national bird, this fruit isn't flightless, and arrives in the UK on long-haul flights but they are hardy travellers and lose little nutritional value on the flight.

Note: some children are sensitive to kiwi fruit – introduce a small amount early in the day and monitor for any adverse reaction.

Makes 2–3 servings

25g (1oz) dried prunes, stoned	1 kiwi fruit
	25g (1oz) tofu

Rinse the prunes, checking for any bits of stone or stalk and chop in small pieces.

In a small pan, bring just enough water to cover the prunes to the boil, add the prunes and simmer for 10 minutes until soft and plump.

Peel the kiwi or cut in half and scoop out the flesh with a teaspoon and put into the chopping bowl of a hand blender. Add the tofu and the prunes, and whizz, adding the water the prunes were cooked in as needed, until it is the right texture for your baby.

Tofu, Fennel and Spinach Purée

Tofu is made from soya bean curd, and is a good way to introduce protein into your baby's diet. Soya beans are soaked, crushed and heated to produce soya milk to which a coagulating agent, calcium sulphate or calcium chloride, is added. The soya curd is then pressed to give tofu. Tofu tends be fairly bland in taste and is best used in recipes where flavour is imparted by other ingredients, which is why it works well with fennel and spinach, both of which have strong flavours. At a later stage in your child's diet, firm tofu may be stir- or deep-fried, sautéed or steamed and added to salads or casseroles. As well as having a high protein content, tofu also contains calcium, iron and vitamins B1, B2 and B3.

Makes 1–2 servings

½ fresh fennel bulb (approx. 75g/3oz)	25g (1oz) spinach leaves (preferably baby spinach as it is slightly sweeter)
	75g (3oz) tofu

Wash and finely chop the fennel into approximately 3mm (1/8in) cubes and steam for 5 minutes.

Wash the spinach leaves and add to the fennel. Steam for a further 5 minutes. Drain the tofu and roughly chop. Combine the steamed fennel and spinach with the tofu in the chopping bowl of a hand blender and whizz, if needed, adding a tablespoon of the collected stock in the steamer or boiled water.

Simple Savoury Quinoa Purée

Quinoa has very little flavour of its own so it works well in savoury and sweet dishes. If this is the first time you are introducing tomato, as with other new foods, try a little at a midday meal so you can check for any intolerance. Also note the same care should be taken when introducing raw tomatoes for the first time; even if your baby is fine with cooked tomatoes, some babies (and adults) have an adverse reaction when tomatoes are eaten raw.

Makes 1 serving

15g (³⁄₄oz) quinoa   2–3 cherry tomatoes
25g (1oz) squash (butternut   25g (1oz) courgette
  or red kuri)

Cover the quinoa with water, bring to the boil then simmer for 10 minutes.

Peel the squash and chop into 3mm (¹⁄₈in) dice, then add to the quinoa and simmer for a further 5 minutes until the grains and squash are soft (the quinoa will go transparent).

Whizz the tomatoes and courgette in the chopper attachment of a hand blender to form a coarse paste and pour into the pan. Cook for 5 minutes, stirring frequently. Add a little more water as needed.

Serve as is or give another quick whizz with the blender if your baby isn't ready for the bitty texture.

Quinoa, Rhubarb and Vanilla Purée

Quinoa dates back to 2700 BC in China where it was cultivated for its purgative medicinal purposes, while rhubarb is native to the Incas of South America. Rhubarb is made up of 95 per cent water but is a fair source of potassium, contains small amounts of vitamins and is low in sodium. Rhubarb is also rich in vitamin C, dietary fibre and calcium. Rhubarb stalks can be a little tart so taste and select the sweetest bits. Only the stalks are edible, so don't use the leaves or roots.

Makes 1–2 servings

15g (³⁄₄oz) quinoa   75g (3oz) rhubarb
1cm (¹⁄₂in) vanilla pod

Rinse the quinoa and split open the vanilla pod. Heat both ingredients in a pan with 2–3 tablespoons of water. Bring to the boil, cover and reduce to a simmer for 5–10 minutes.

Slice the rhubarb thinly and stir into the mix. Simmer for 8–10 minutes until the grains are transparent and the rhubarb soft. Whizz in the chopping bowl of a blender.

Tip If the rhubarb is particularly tart, stir in a couple of teaspoons of a sweeter purée such as pear, apple or peach.

Minty Pea and Potato Purée

A refreshing combo, peas contain protein but not all the essential amino acids, so for more information, see page 17.

Makes 1–2 servings

75g (3oz) potato
  or sweet potato
50g (2oz) fresh or frozen peas

2–3 leaves of fresh mint (or
  pinch of dried)

Wash, peel and finely chop or grate the potato. If using fresh peas, rinse with the mint leaves. Steam both ingredients for 10 minutes. Alternatively bring to the boil just enough water to cover the ingredients, add the ingredients and simmer gently. Check the largest piece of potato is soft then blend to the right texture for your baby.

When serving ensure all the whole peas have been mashed. If not, squash with the back of a spoon before giving to your baby.

Beetroot, Apple and Butterbean Purée

Makes 1–2 servings

1 small beetroot (approx
  50g/2oz)
½ medium dessert apple

50g (2oz) butterbeans
  (tinned, in water, or
  prepared as instructed on
  packet)

Wash and peel the beetroot and chop into 3mm (¹/₈in) dice, and heat in a pan with 2 tablespoons of boiling water.

Wash, core and peel the apple then grate into the simmering beetroot. Simmer for a further 8 minutes.

Rinse the butterbeans and add to the mix and simmer for a further 2 minutes to heat through.

Give the mix a quick whizz with the hand blender to make a slightly textured purée.

*Nappy warning! See page 66.

Chicken for Beginners

Makes 2–3 servings

100g (3$\frac{1}{2}$oz) chicken fillet, skinless

$\frac{1}{2}$ red pepper (approx 50g/2oz)
$\frac{1}{4}$ avocado (approx 50g/2oz)

Wash and dice the chicken and red pepper into small cubes. Steam the chicken and pepper for 8–10 minutes, checking the chicken is cooked thoroughly.

Whizz the chicken and pepper with 1–2 tablespoons of stock (from the steamer) or boiled water.

Divide the mix into two and set aside half the mix to freeze (avocado doesn't freeze very well so it should be added just before serving).

Roughly chop the avocado, add to the chicken and pepper purée and whizz with a hand blender to a slightly textured purée.

Tip Keep the stone in the unused avocado – this will reduce the discolouration.

Chicken, Leek and Sweetcorn

Makes 1 serving

25g (1oz) leek
40g (1$\frac{1}{2}$oz) chicken breast, skinless
2 teaspoons olive oil
50g (2oz) carrot

40g (1$\frac{1}{2}$oz) potato or sweet potato
2 baby sweetcorn
1 tablespoon baby's usual milk

Finely chop the leek, rinse the chicken and cut into small cubes. Heat the oil in a small saucepan and gently fry so the leek softens and the chicken cooks but does not brown. Check the largest piece of chicken has cooked through.

Wash, peel and dice or grate the carrot and sweet potato, dice the baby corn and stir into the pan. Add 1–2 tablespoons of water and the milk, cover and simmer for 8 minutes.

Whizz with a hand blender or push through a mouli to get the right consistency for your baby – as your baby becomes more confident, you will not need to blend.

First Fish Stew

Makes 1 serving

25g (1oz) carrot
25g (1oz) potato
25g (1oz) swede
25g (1oz) broccoli

1 sprig of fresh parsley
  (optional)
25g (1oz) white fish fillet
  (skinless)

Wash and peel the carrot, potato and swede and grate or cut into 3mm ($\frac{1}{8}$in) dice. Wash and trim the broccoli and parsley (if using) and finely chop by hand or in the chopper attachment of a hand blender.

Wash the fish and cut into small cubes, removing any bits of bone. Put all the ingredients into a small saucepan and add just enough water to cover. Bring to the boil then cover and reduce to a simmer for 12 minutes until the largest piece is soft and the fish flakes into the mix. This can gently simmer for longer if you wish, bringing out the flavour as it reduces; just make sure to add enough water or a little of your baby's usual milk as needed.

Salmon, Broccoli, Cauliflower and Potato Purée

A quick and easy way to introduce fish is to use a recipe you know your baby likes and mash in the steamed fish.
Makes 1 serving

50g (2oz) broccoli
50g (2oz) cauliflower
60g (2½oz) potato

25g (1oz) salmon fillet,
  skinless

Follow the Broccoli, Cauliflower and Potato Purée recipe on page 87 or defrost a pot of ready-made purée.

Rinse the salmon fillet and dice into small cubes, checking as you cut for any small bits of bone. Steam for 8–10 minutes, making sure the largest piece is cooked right through.

Mash with a fork and stir into the purée, adding some of the steamer tray stock.

Tip The tail end of fish has less bone; explain to the fishmonger that it's for your baby and ask for a tail fillet.

Broccoli and Peas with Cheese

Your baby's first cheese experience – choose one that melts well such as cheddar or edam and don't forget mild, hard goat's cheese.

Makes 1 serving

40g (1½oz) potato
50g (2oz) broccoli

40g (1½oz) fresh or frozen peas
15g (¾oz) mild hard cheese

Wash and peel the potato and trim and finely chop the broccoli. Bring 3 tablespoons of water to the boil and add the finely chopped broccoli, return to the boil and reduce to a gentle simmer.

Dice the potato into 3mm (⅛in) cubes or grate into the broccoli and add the peas. Cover and simmer for 10–12 minutes until all the pieces are soft.

Mash well or push through a mouli. While still hot, grate in the cheese and stir as it melts into the purée.

Eggy Mash

Most children love eggs which is great because they are a nutritional marvel. Wait until 9 months – towards the end of stage 2 – before you try this recipe. I've put Eggy Mash in this section because it's a very easy way to separate the white and yolk. Why? Some people are sensitive to the white and others to the yolk – so try Eggy Mash first with just the yolk as this is the least problematic, then the next time with just the white – if there is no reaction to either you'll know that you're fine with the beaten-egg recipes in stage 3.

I would urge you to select organic free-range eggs, even if you are not convinced about organic the rest of the time.

Makes 1 serving

75g (3oz) potato or sweet potato or 3–4 cubes of purée
1 egg – you will only need part of it

1 dessertspoon of your baby's usual milk

Wash, peel and chop the potato and steam or boil so that it is mashable.

Meanwhile hardboil an egg for 10 minutes, then remove and run under the cold tap until the egg is cool enough to peel. Peel and quarter the egg. Mash half the yolk or a quarter of the white in with the potato, adding the milk to make it creamy.

Serve at the right temperature for your baby in a morning or daytime feed, giving you the rest of the day to monitor any reactions.

Note Always ensure eggs are thoroughly cooked for a child under 12 months.

The first Christmas

Congratulations! This is your little cracker's first Christmas, so make sure they're not feeling left out by giving them these festive treats. Party hats and streamers are optional, for you that is!

Sweet Potato, Parsnip, Carrot, Onion and Sage Mash

I prefer this steamed together as it seems to infuse the flavours – it can also be prepared by simmering together in a pan.

Makes 1 serving

40g (1½oz) sweet potato
40g (1½oz) parsnip
40g (1½oz) carrot
10g (½oz) onion

2–3 sage leaves
A little of your baby's usual milk

Wash and peel the sweet potato, parsnip, carrot and onion and grate or dice into 3mm (⅛in) cubes. Rinse and chop the sage.

Mix together and steam for 10–12 minutes.

Mash with a little of your baby's usual milk and the stock from the steamer tray.

Plum and Prune Pudding

Not quite Christmas pudding but seasonal enough to feel that your baby is joining in their first Christmas celebration. Older kids not convinced by the delights of Christmas pud may also like this as is or with yogurt or ice cream.

Makes 1 serving

3 ready-to-eat prunes, stoned
1 ripe plum or 2–3 cubes of plum purée

2 teaspoons millet flakes or fine oat flakes
Pinch of cinnamon (optional)

Chop the prunes into approximately 3mm (⅛in) dice and simmer for 2 minutes in 2 tablespoons of water.

Peel the plum (see Peach, Plum and Vanilla Purée on page 91) and remove the stone. Chop and add to the prunes and sprinkle in the millet or oat flakes and cinnamon, if using, stirring to avoid lumps.

Cook for 2–3 minutes, stirring frequently, until it thickens, then whizz with a hand blender until it is the right consistency for your baby.

Week 6+: New Tastes and Nutritional Building Blocks

Some babies love variety, others prefer a more steady approach – it's fine to repeat one day's plan the following day, and you might find it easier to manage too. By the same token, remember to try out some new recipes now and then as it can be easy to get stuck in a favourite food rut. Remember to include a drink of water with mealtimes.

At this stage the principle is to introduce a protein-rich lunch. Particularly hungry babies may need a stop-gap between breakfast and lunch or as a dessert after dinner – a little yogurt and fruit purée is ideal.

The volume of breast or formula milk needed depends on age and weight, so vary accordingly.

	Wake-up	Breakfast	Lunch	Mid-afternoon	Dinner	Supper	Bedtime (optional)
Day 1	Breast milk or formula milk (about 220m/8fl oz)	No-gluten Muesli (see p85)	Squash and Red Lentil Purée (see p99) Kiwi, Prune and Tofu Purée (see p100)	Breast milk or formula milk (about 180ml/6fl oz)	Potato, Parsnip and Pear Purée (see p87)	Breast milk or formula milk (about 200ml/7fl oz)	Breast milk or formula milk (about 50ml/2fl oz)*
Day 2	Breast milk or formula milk (about 220m/8fl oz)	Banana and Prune Purée (see p84)	Chicken for Beginners (see p104) Apple and Mango Purée (see p96)	Breast milk or formula milk (about 180ml/6fl oz)	Minty Pea and Potato Purée (see p103)	Breast milk or formula milk (about 200ml/7fl oz)	Breast milk or formula milk (about 50ml/2fl oz)*
Day 3	Breast milk or formula milk (about 220m/8fl oz)	Millet and Fruits (see p84)	Tofu, Fennel and Spinach Purée (see p100) Apple and Pear Purée (see p96)	Breast milk or formula milk (about 180ml/6fl oz)	Carrot and Sweet Potato Purée (see p86)	Breast milk or formula milk (about 200ml/7fl oz)	Breast milk or formula milk (about 50ml/2fl oz)*
Day 4	Breast milk or formula milk (about 220m/8fl oz)	Beginner's Porridge (see p84)	First Fish Stew (see p106) Mango with Blackberry Ripple (see p95)	Breast milk or formula milk (about 180ml/6fl oz)	Broccoli, Cauliflower and Potato Purée (see p87)	Breast milk or formula milk (about 200ml/7fl oz)	Breast milk or formula milk (about 50ml/2fl oz)*
Day 5	Breast milk or formula milk (about 220m/8fl oz)	No-gluten Muesli (see p85)	Chicken, Leek and Sweetcorn (see p104) Peach, Plum and Vanilla Purée (see p91)	Breast milk or formula milk (about 180ml/6fl oz)	Pea and Bean Purée (see p88)	Breast milk or formula milk (about 200ml/7fl oz)	Breast milk or formula milk (about 50ml/2fl oz)*
Day 6	Breast milk or formula milk (about 220m/8fl oz)	Banana and Prune Purée (see p84)	Squash and Red Lentil Purée (see p99) Quinoa, Rhubarb and Vanilla Purée (see p102)	Breast milk or formula milk (about 180ml/6fl oz)	Spinach and Sweet Potato Purée (see p88)	Breast milk or formula milk (about 200ml/7fl oz)	Breast milk or formula milk (about 50ml/2fl oz)*
Day 7	Breast milk or formula milk (about 220m/8fl oz)	Millet and Fruits (see p84)	Salmon, Broccoli, Cauliflower and Potato Purée (see p106) Nectarine & Dried Apricot Purée (see p92)	Breast milk or formula milk (about 180ml/6fl oz)	Leek, Carrot and Potato Purée (see p88)	Breast milk or formula milk (about 200ml/7fl oz)	Breast milk or formula milk (about 50ml/2fl oz)*

* Optional, although many babies find it a comforting part of their bedtime routine

Stage three:
Independent weaning

They're beginning to become comfortable with feeding themselves.
This section is a pick 'n' mix selection of bite-size recipes they can get
their sticky paws into.

The third stage

Freedom, movement… and an opinion of their own. Your baby is changing daily and turning from a baby to a mini person before your eyes. Their hand–eye co-ordination is developing at a rapid rate and so is their sense of cause and effect. Using cutlery is a huge step and you may find your little clever clogs will delight in trying to feed you (which is fair play, since you've been feeding them). It's time to swap those weaning spoons for child-friendly cutlery, buying one set for your baby and one for you. Your baby should be 9–12 months old before you move onto this stage.

Letting your baby learn to feed themselves is a messy business. Cover the floor with a clean plastic mat which you can easily scrape food off (the mat needs to be cleaned and dried every time).

At this stage, their fingers seem to be picking up and feeling everything. It's no surprise that your baby will love finger food. After all, babies are sensual beings and enjoying the sight, sound and feel of food as much as the way it tastes is one of life's great pleasures. Finger foods help with the all-important skills of biting, chewing and self-feeding. Remember to keep the food soft and an easy size to hold, ensuring there are no pips, stones or bones. Relaxed finger-food meals like sandwiches and pizza slices are easy for the evenings.

After a couple of months of eating more mashed food, your baby will be getting the hang of chewing, so it's time to introduce coarser bits. Even if your baby doesn't have many teeth, you'll be surprised how effective their gums are. The goal is slowly to introduce more solid, chewable foods until solid food is the main meal. Start with lightly cooked veg or bite-sized pieces of soft fruit. Next try raw, grated vegetables and finely chopped salads. Introduce new textures every two days and start to vary temperatures, serving some foods warm and others cold.

As your baby devours more solids, they'll drink less milk; if your baby isn't getting a taste for solids at this stage it may be a good idea to reduce their milk intake slightly so that they're hungry for solids. Milk is still important, although much of their calcium can come from solid dairy products in foods like hard cheese, fromage frais, milk puddings and yogurts. Remember, in order to digest calcium, your baby will need vitamin D, boron, magnesium and manganese. While dairy is an important source of calcium, don't forget that non-dairy sources, like broccoli, can have more. Other good sources of calcium include sardines, salmon and egg yolks.

Your baby will now be enjoying three good meals a day and it's time to make them more adventurous. In a day, your baby should be eating around 3–4 servings of carbohydrates, at least 1 serving of a meat or fish protein or, if you're raising a veggie baby, 2 servings of a vegetable protein. A baby also needs 3–4 portions of fruit and vegetables, working up to the adult 5-a-day.

Start introducing foods with stronger flavours, like aubergines, mushrooms, pineapple, olives and citrus fruits. Introduce them slowly and one at a time, so you watch for any allergic reactions. You can also introduce wheat if you haven't already done so.

Mess and attitude

Your child is nearly walking or crawling and all of sudden they've got more attitude than Eminem. So what's the problem? Bottom line is that life's pretty frustrating at this age. Since they were born they've heard words, and slowly they should be starting to make sense of them. But as yet they can't quite get their message across. Their wah, nah, goo conversations will make perfect sense to them, but unfortunately not to you, so when you remove a toy or a doll their verbal volley won't quite get the response they intend, so cue hysterical waterworks. They're probably used to having a small entourage, i.e. you, so don't be surprised if when you hand them over to Granny, a friend or a helper you get the serious diva treatment. They will also be prepared to put anything up their nose or down their throat, so make sure that small, round or sharp objects – anything that could cause choking – are locked away in a secure cupboard or discarded.

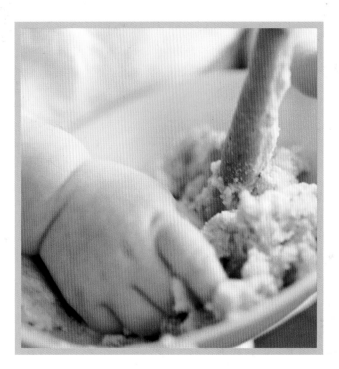

Be prepared

If you are the sort of person who likes everything neat, tidy and in its correct place, take a deep breath now, because at this age everything goes out the window – quite often literally! Your child has an appetite for destruction and flinging a piece of food across the room and watching it slide down the fridge is damn good fun. If you're in the firing line don't take it personally. What was it Mum used to say?, 'Patience is a virtue,' so count to 3. It's not just food that will get the slam-dunk treatment – expect toys and cutlery to whizz around as well, so don't give them the chance. If you're going to arm yourself with anything go for springy cutlery (see the photograph on page 111). This is a great invention because after attaching the suckers to their dining area you can sit back and relax as they fling the cutlery away and it returns like a boomerang.

The most important thing to understand at this age is that your child is not trying to question your authority and doesn't have the cognitive ability to play mind games, so when they seemingly misbehave it's not a slight on you; it's just their way of expressing themselves. So try to enjoy this period because before you know it you'll have to deal with a real-life walking, talking-living doll.

Choking

In cases of choking, follow the steps below:
- Do not attempt to retrieve the object with your fingers as this can push it further down the windpipe.
- Place your baby head down along your forearm and give four sharp slaps across the top of the back between the shoulder blades. If this fails turn the baby over and on to your lap. Give a few sharp thrusts on the lower breast bone using two fingers.
- If unsuccessful, repeat these measures and call emergency services.

Breakfast

Some independent babies become frustrated if they cannot feed themselves and you try to spoon-feed them. Try these recipes if your baby is insisting on finger foods or if you feel like adding some variety into their breakfast diet. Some of these recipes contain whole milk. Uncooked whole milk should not be given to babies under 12 months.

French Toast

Most French toast recipes add sugar and then smother with loads of honey or maple syrup. Honey is still a no-no until 12 months so this recipe uses the natural sweetness of apple juice. Serve with bite-sized pieces of fresh fruit.

Makes approx 20 cubes – enough for baby and 1 adult (not suitable for freezing)

1 medium egg
50ml (2$\frac{1}{2}$fl oz) apple juice
$\frac{1}{4}$–$\frac{1}{2}$ teaspoon ground cinnamon
15g ($\frac{3}{4}$oz) butter

1 soft bread roll – preferably wholemeal (to make your own see No-salt Breadsticks dough recipe on page 126)
Selection of your child's favourite fresh fruit

Beat the egg until slightly fluffy. Add the apple juice and cinnamon and beat again.

Heat the butter in a non-stick frying pan. Trim the bread roll of any hard or crispy crust and cut into bite-sized pieces (approx 1$\frac{1}{2}$cm/$\frac{3}{4}$in cubes).

Coat the bread cubes in the egg mix (aim to coat rather than soak). Very fresh bread will take up the mix quickly and go soggy, so try one cube first to test. Place the cubes in the pan and cook until golden on each side.

Dust with a little extra cinnamon and serve with finger-food pieces of fresh fruit.

Plum and Porridge Pancakes

Finger food is easier than trying to manoeuvre a spoon but porridge as a finger food can start the day off in a sticky mess. This recipe is inspired by American-style pancakes, but avoids using self-raising flour or baking powder as both are too high in sodium for babies under 12 months (for older children a more traditional recipe can be found on page 145).

Makes 4 mini pancakes /1–2 servings
(not suitable for freezing)

1 rounded tablespoon rolled (porridge) oats	1 small plum, stoned (or other favourite fresh fruit)
1 rounded tablespoon plain flour	15g (¾oz) butter or margarine
1 tablespoon whole milk	½ medium egg*

Whizz the rolled oats using the chopping attachment of a hand blender to form a coarse oat flour. Combine with the flour in a small mixing bowl and add the milk to form a thick batter. Wash and coarsely chop the plum (also works well with blueberries, banana or apple).

Heat the butter in a large non-stick frying pan.

Beat the egg until it has at least doubled in volume. When thick and stiff, fold into the oat batter, then finally stir through the fruit pieces.

Use a dessertspoon to measure out the mix for each pancake – they should spread to around 6cm (2½in) across. Cook on each side for 2 minutes until golden and cooked through.

Cut into small pieces as appropriate for your baby.

If you require a wheat-free version, replace the plain flour with an extra spoonful of oats (this will make a slightly heavier pancake).

*Rather than half an egg going to waste, double the quantities and make enough for the family. Although this recipe doesn't freeze, it will keep covered in the fridge for 24 hours – so simply toast or grill to reheat for the following day or as a tea-time treat for older children or adults.

Cheese Dreams

Cheese Dreams was my grandma's grandiose name for eggy cheese sarnies! They are similar to French toast – but savoury.

Makes 1–2 servings (16 mini triangles)
(not suitable for freezing)

15g (¾oz) butter	1 small egg
1 slice wholemeal bread	Freshly ground black pepper
25g (1oz) hard mild cheese	

Use a tiny amount of the butter to spread on the bread (it will help the sandwich stay together until the cheese melts). Slice the cheese and make a triangular sandwich with the bread and cut in half and half again until you have four mini triangles.

Beat the egg with the black pepper until slightly fluffy and heat the remaining butter in a non-stick frying pan. Dip the triangles in the egg to coat and slightly soak, then pan cook for 3 minutes on each side until golden, making sure the egg is thoroughly cooked and the cheese melted.

Stocks

Some recipes suggest using a stock, but commercial stock usually has added salt and can contain flavour enhancers. In particular, avoid stock cubes and powders that are both high in salt and contain monosodium glutamate (MSG). Stock is easy to make and can be made in batches and frozen in small pots or ice-cube trays. It's handy as a base for soup, to gently flavour rice and to add depth of flavour to many recipes, but if time is not on your side all the recipes will work with water in place of the stock.

Basic Vegetable Stock

Makes about 1 litre (1¾ pints)

1 large carrot
40g (1½oz) leek
1 medium onion
40g (1½oz) celery
1 garlic clove (optional)
1 bay leaf
1½ litres (2½ pints) water

Wash and roughly chop the vegetables and slice the garlic (this will give a milder taste than crushing).

Put all the ingredients in a large pan with the water and bring to the boil. Cover and simmer gently for about 1 hour. The volume of the stock will reduce by about a third, giving a greater intensity of flavour. Use a slotted spoon to remove the vegetable pieces, then push through a fine sieve. Cover and allow to cool, then freeze in small pots or ice-cube trays.

Fish, Meat or Poultry Stock

The leftovers from a roast dinner are perfect for making stock – include any meat (but not fat) trimmings, but avoid skin that has been salted or seasoned.

Makes about 1 litre (1¾ pints)

1 large carrot
40g (1½oz) leek or 1 medium onion
40g (1½oz) celery
1 bay leaf or sprig of fresh parsley
1½ litres (2½ pints) water
1–2 grilled trout carcass (bones and head) or cooked bones and meat trimmings (but not fat) from a roast dinner

Wash and chop the vegetables. Put all the ingredients in a large pan with the water and bring to the boil. Cover and simmer gently for about 1 hour until the volume of the stock reduces by about a third. If there is lot of fat on top of the stock quickly drop in, then scoop out a couple of ice cubes (have a slotted spoon at the ready) – you will find that the fat clings to the cube and solidifies.

Remove the largest pieces with a slotted spoon then strain through a paper coffee filter or very fine sieve to ensure that no small bones end up in the finished stock. Cover and allow to cool, then freeze in small pots or ice-cube trays.

Fish

Fish is a superb protein and contains calcium, magnesium, and selenium. Oily varieties, like mackerel, salmon and tuna, are full of Omega 3 and 6 fatty acids, crucial for brain development. Tuna scores high in the vitamin B3, B12 and D stakes, while salmon is full of potassium and magnesium. If buying fresh, choose fish that smells fresh not fishy; the eyes should look bright and clear and the flesh should be springy. Frozen fish is equally nutritious, and possibly fresher, if frozen at sea. If buying tinned fish, choose fish packed in olive oil, sunflower oil or water, not in brine.

Eggy Herby Fish Bites

This recipe containing egg and salmon gives a double whammy of brain-building Omega–3.
Makes 1–2 servings (not suitable for freezing)

¼–½ **teaspoon mild fresh herbs (e.g. parsley, dill)**
1 small egg
Small pinch of finely ground black pepper
1 teaspoon olive oil
50g (2oz) skinless salmon or white fish

Wash and finely chop the herbs, then, in a small mixing bowl, beat into the egg and add the pepper.

Heat the oil in a non-stick frying pan.

Wash and pat dry the fish with kitchen paper, then cut into bite sized cubes, removing all bits of fish bone as you go. Put the fish in the egg mix and coat thoroughly. Use a teaspoon to place the coated fish into the pan, ensuring that there is a space between each piece to avoid clumping. Spoon any extra egg mix over the fish pieces. Cook for 2–3 minutes on each side until browned and thoroughly cooked through.

For a simpler recipe, omit the herbs. Serve with rice or steamed potatoes.

Fisherman's Pie

Makes 1 serving

1 medium potato or sweet potato (approx. 175g/6oz)
2 teaspoons olive oil
25g (1oz) onion or leek
75g (3oz) skinned fish (white or salmon)
25g (1oz) baby sweetcorn
25g (1oz) carrots
25g (1oz) peas
1 tablespoon water
1 dessertspoon crème fraîche or ½ tablespoon whole milk
2 teaspoons whole milk
10g (½ oz) mild hard cheese, grated (optional)

Preheat the oven to 200°C/400°F/gas mark 6. Wash, peel and chop the potato and boil or steam until soft. Drain and set aside.

Heat the olive oil in a medium-sized saucepan. Finely chop the onion or leek and sauté.

Rinse the fish, check for bones and chop into 1cm (½in) cubes. Chop the baby sweetcorn and carrot. Add the sweetcorn, carrot, peas and fish to the onion and cook for 3 minutes. Stir in the water and crème fraîche.

Mash the potato with the milk.

Pour the fish mix into a small ovenproof dish. Top with mashed potato and cheese. Bake for 20 minutes until the top is slightly browned. Serve.

Tuna Rice

Whether in sandwiches, pasta or salad, tuna has become a staple of most adults' diets – oily fish is rich in vitamin B12, D, Omega 3 and, of course, protein. This recipe introduces tuna to your baby for the first time. It needs very little fish – so treat yourself to the rest in a salad or bake. Note, if using tinned tuna, choose tuna packed in spring water or oil but not in brine as even when drained this will be too salty for your little one.

Makes 1 serving

(This recipe can be frozen but cooked rice should not be stored at room temperature – use immediately once defrosted.)

25g (1oz) long-grain rice
50g (2oz) fresh tuna (drained, if using tinned; see note above)
25g (1oz) courgette
25g (1oz) mushrooms
25g (1oz) yellow or orange pepper
½ garlic clove, crushed (optional)
2–3 cherry tomatoes
1 teaspoon olive oil
1 teaspoon natural yogurt or whole milk (optional)

Steam or boil the rice until soft, drain and set aside.

If using fresh tuna, wash and chop the tuna. Then chop the courgette, mushrooms, pepper, garlic and tomatoes into ½cm (¼in) cubes. Steam the tuna and vegetables for 8 minutes. Alternatively, heat the oil in a small saucepan and gently cook the tuna with the garlic, if using. Add the vegetables and continue to cook for 3–4 minutes until the tuna is cooked through.

Stir in the rice, adding the milk or yogurt, if liked, to give a creamy finish.

Fish Creole

This mix of fruit, fish and vegetables will become a firm favourite with children and grown-ups, especially for those who are not very keen on the flavour of fish on its own.

Makes 2–3 servings

1 tablespoon olive oil
½ medium onion (approx. 100g/3½oz)
1 garlic clove
25g (1oz) fresh ginger root (reduce to suit your child)
200g (7oz) ripe tomatoes (or tin of organic plum tomatoes)
100g (3½oz) fresh pineapple (or tinned in natural juice)
100g (3½oz) red pepper
50g (2oz) green pepper
150g (5oz) white fish, without skin or bones
Juice of 1 lime (optional)
Pinch of chilli powder (optional)
Freshly ground black pepper

Warm the olive oil in a large frying pan. Finely chop the onion, crush the garlic and finely chop the ginger or crush (if you have a robust garlic press). Gently cook the onion, garlic and ginger until the onion softens. Do not brown. Chop the tomatoes, pineapple and peppers into bite-sized pieces and add to the onion, garlic and ginger mix. Gently simmer for 5 minutes.

Wash and thoroughly check the fish for bones (you may find it useful to have a pair of kitchen tweezers to pull out the more stubborn bones).

Chop the fish into bite-sized chunks and add to the frying pan. Either add 1 tablespoon of water or the lime juice, the chilli powder, if using, and black pepper. Cover the pan and cook for 5–10 minutes until the fish is opaque and cooked through.

Serve with boiled rice or noodles.

Chicken

A skinned, boned breast, which is the leanest part of the chicken, has less than half the fat of a steak. Chicken is a primary protein, packed with all eight essential amino acids as well as an abundance of vitamins A, B3, B6 and B12. Choose organic chicken as free-range chickens may roam freely, but can also be stuffed with hormones and antibiotics. Organic chickens are fed an organically grown diet and are able to wander about doing whatever chickens do.

Grandma Daisy's Casserole

It may be a bit extravagant to put the oven on for just one portion, so either prepare this when you have the oven on already or multiply up and make a batch to freeze or feed the rest of the family.
Makes 1–2 servings

50g (2oz) skinless chicken breast or lean beef or lamb
25g (1oz) leek
1 teaspoon olive oil or butter
50g (2oz) carrot
50g (2oz) potato
50g (2oz) turnip or swede

100ml (3½fl oz) salt-free stock (see page 118) or water
1 small bay leaf (optional)
1 teaspoon parsley, chives or thyme (optional)

Preheat the oven to 150°C/300°F/gas mark 2.

Wash and dice the meat and cut into bite-sized cubes. Wash and slice the leek.

Heat the oil or butter in a small saucepan and cook the chicken and leek until they begin to brown. Place in a small ovenproof dish.

Wash, peel and cube the carrot, potato and turnip or swede and add to the chicken and leek mix. Pour over the stock or water, sprinkle with the herbs and add the bay leaf, if using, and stir. Cover with foil and cook for 40 minutes to 1 hour. Stir halfway through, adding a little more water if needed. Remember to remove the bay leaf before serving.

Chicken Curry

Makes 1 serving

1 teaspoon olive oil
25g (1oz) leek or onion
1 small garlic clove (optional)
50g (2oz) skinless chicken breast or mince
¼–½ teaspoon garam masala

25g (1oz) carrot
40g (1½oz) potato
25g (1oz) apple
4–5 sultanas
50ml (2fl oz) salt-free stock (see page 118) or water

Heat the oil, finely chop the leek or onion, crush the garlic, if using, and add to the oil.

Rinse and cut the chicken into bite-sized cubes, sprinkle with the garam masala and add to the pan. Stir until the chunks are cooked through.

Wash and peel the carrot, potato and apple, and cut the sultanas in half if necessary. Add to the pan, together with the stock and simmer for 10–15 minutes until the potatoes are cooked.

Sweet and Sour Chicken

Makes 1 serving

1 teaspoon olive oil
2–3 spring onions
50g (2oz) skinless chicken
  breast
40g (1½oz) pak choi, green
  beans or mangetout
1 small tomato

50g (2oz) pineapple or mango
2–3 baby sweetcorn
1 dessertspoon rice
1 tablespoon pineapple juice
2 tablespoons salt-free stock
  (see page 118) or water

Heat the oil in a non-stick frying pan. Slice the spring onions, cube the chicken and add to the pan. Cook until slightly browned, then reduce to a low heat.

Wash and chop the vegetables and fruit and add to the pan. Increase the heat and bring back to a gentle simmer. Stir in the rice, juice and stock and simmer until the rice is soft.

Tip For older children add a little tomato purée, Worcester sauce or cider vinegar to bring out the sourness.

Chicken Bites

Makes 1–2 servings

2 teaspoons olive oil
½ egg, beaten
2 teaspoons cornflour or
  wholemeal plain flour

50g (2oz) skinless chicken
  breast

Heat the olive oil in a non-stick frying pan. Beat the egg and gradually stir into the flour to form a simple batter.

Rinse and cut the chicken into bite-sized cubes. Dip the cubes in the batter and stir to coat.

Pan fry the chicken for about 2 minutes on each side until golden brown and both the egg and chicken are thoroughly cooked through.

Meat

Anaemia is a condition caused by a shortage of iron and leads to tiredness, physical lethargy and a lowered IQ. As your baby's iron stores become depleted at around 6 months, this is something to be aware of. Enter iron-rich foods. Enter meat. Meat is a high-quality protein coloured red by the myoglobin, an oxygen-storing pigment that houses iron: the redder the meat, the more myoglobin and therefore the more iron it will have. Red meat also has vast riches of the vitamin B family. A serving of lamb, for example, contains more than the recommended daily allowance (RDA) for B12 as well as trace elements of copper, manganese and selenium. When purchasing meat, look for lean, organic cuts to avoid the antibiotics and hormones added to non-organic meats.

Mini Meatballs

Makes 8 meatballs

50g (2oz) lean mince (beef, lamb, turkey or chicken)
1 tablespoon fresh wholemeal breadcrumbs

15g (¾oz) onion
1 teaspoon olive oil

Put the minced meat, breadcrumbs and onion into the chopping bowl of a hand blender and whizz until smooth.

Measure out teaspoons of the mix and roll into round, even, bite-sized balls.

Heat a teaspoon of olive oil in a non-stick pan and gently fry the meatballs until brown. Serve with sauce (see page 125).

Tip If your child is not yet ready for whole meatballs, simply mash into the sauce with a fork

Meatball Sauce

Makes 2–3 servings

1 teaspoon olive oil	1–2 tablespoons water
15g (³⁄₄oz) red onion	25g (1oz) red pepper
25g (1oz) carrot	1 small ripe tomato (about
25g (1oz) sweet potato	75g/3oz)
7–15g (¹⁄₄–³⁄₄oz) fresh	2 teaspoons whole milk
beetroot or beetroot purée	
(page 66)	

Heat the olive oil in a small saucepan. Finely chop the onion and gently cook.

Wash, peel and finely chop the carrot and sweet potato (if using fresh beetroot, peel and finely chop and add here) and add to the onion. Cook for a further 3 minutes then add the water and gently simmer.

Wash and chop the red pepper and tomato and add to the pan together with the milk. Bring to the boil and simmer for a further 4 minutes. If using beetroot purée, stir through a little at a time to colour the sauce to the desired red. Whizz with a hand blender until it is the appropriate texture for your child.

Quick meatball sauce method: if you have frozen cubes of purées, simply sweat the onion with the olive oil and add a frozen cube each of carrot and sweet potato purée, and 1 cube of beetroot purée. Heat until defrosted. Wash and finely chop the tomato and red pepper and stir in with the milk (and, if needed, additional water). Blend as before.

Goulash

The traditional Hungarian recipe typically has lashings of paprika and cayenne pepper. This is somewhat milder although quite a lot of young children enjoy a bit of spice – especially if breastfed by a mum who loves spicy foods. Vary the quantities to suit the preference of your child.

This recipe introduces aubergine – as with all new foods, try a little first to check for any allergic reaction before making up large batches.

Makes 1 serving

50g (2oz) lean beef, lamb or	Large pinch of paprika
chicken	A little freshly ground black
¹⁄₂ small onion	pepper
1 teaspoon olive oil	75ml (3fl oz) salt-free stock
25g (1oz) green pepper	(see page 118)
25g (1oz) aubergine	1 dessertspoon rice
1 small ripe tomato	Pinch of cayenne pepper
1 garlic clove	(optional for an older child)

Chop the meat into bite-sized cubes and finely chop the onion.

Heat the olive oil in a saucepan and slightly brown the meat with the onion. Wash, chop and add all the other ingredients except the stock and rice and stir continuously until they start to sizzle. Pour in the stock and rice, bring to the boil and simmer, stirring occasionally, until the rice is soft, adding a little more stock or water if needed.

For an older child, add a little pinch of cayenne pepper and more paprika before adding the rice.

Taking a dip

Using raw vegetables or a breadstick may not seem such a major step but for a baby this is one giant leap into the world of cutlery and eating like an adult. Also these recipes save on cooking time if you've got friends coming round.

No-salt Breadsticks

Breadsticks are handy for dipping into sweet and savoury purées and are a good way to introduce a child to the idea of cutlery. They also make great teething sticks for your baby.

The same dough recipe can be used as a pizza base as well as bread rolls for burgers and buns.

Makes approx. 40 breadsticks

100g (3½oz) strong wholemeal flour
3g fast-acting dried yeast (most fast-acting yeasts do not require sugar to be added – read the instructions on the packet to check and add accordingly)
100ml (3½fl oz) hand-hot water (mix 75ml/3fl oz hot water with 25ml/½oz cold)
2 teaspoons olive oil

Preheat the oven to 220°C/425°F/gas mark 7.

Combine the flour and yeast in a mixing bowl. Pour in the water and oil and use your fingers to make a dough.

Lightly flour a clean work surface and knead for 5 minutes. Divide the mix into two, cover half with a lightly oiled piece of clingfilm to prevent it drying out and set aside. Roll the remaining dough into a long sausage approximately 5mm (¼in) in diameter and cut into mini breadstick lengths (approx. 7cm/2¾in).

Lay on a lightly oiled baking tray and bake for 20–25 minutes until golden and crisp (they should not be soft as they will not keep). Repeat for the remaining dough.

Allow to cool and store in an airtight container for up to 1 week.

Baby-friendly Hummus (Chickpea Purée)

Chickpeas may be small but they're a rich source of protein, carbohydrate, B-group vitamins and monounsaturated fats. They are digested slowly so help to stabilise blood sugar levels and aid the slow release of sugar into the bloodstream. They are also perfect for parents bringing up their babies on a vegan or vegetarian diet.

Hummus is traditionally made with tahini – a sesame-seed-based paste, but it is best to wait until your child is older before giving them seeds. Shop-bought hummus can also be high in salt and other additives. This simplified hummus is a great dipping purée as it's sticky enough to stay put on the breadsticks or crudités.

½ medium onion (100g/3½oz)
1–2 garlic cloves (depending on the taste of your child)
1–2 tablespoons olive oil
150g (5oz) tinned chickpeas (tinned in water, not brine)
Juice of ¼ lemon or lime (optional)
¼ teaspoon paprika (optional)

Finely chop the onion and crush the garlic. Heat 1 tablespoon of olive oil in a non-stick frying pan and gently cook the onion and garlic until soft but not brown. Drain and rinse the chickpeas and combine with the onion, garlic and optional extras in the chopping attachment of a hand blender. Whizz until smooth. Add a little additional olive oil and a tablespoon of water to create a smooth glossy paste.

Serve with breadsticks and baby-sized crudités.

Cheesy Broccoli, Cauliflower and Potato Dip

Makes 1 serving

1 portion of Broccoli, Cauliflower and Potato Purée (see page 87)	15–25g (¾–1oz) mild hard cheese

If using frozen purée, defrost and heat in a saucepan or microwave. Grate the cheese and stir in until melted. Serve with No-salt Breadsticks (see page 126).

Most of the stage 2 purées can also be used as dips just as they are or add herbs, grated cheese or a little natural yogurt for variety.

Avocado Dip

Makes 1 serving

¼–½ ripe avocado	1 dessertspoon natural yogurt

Simply mash the avocado into the yogurt and serve with No-salt Breadsticks (see page 126) and steamed crudités (see right).

Herby Crème Fraîche with Steamed Crudités

Makes 1 serving

1–2 teaspoons fresh herbs, e.g. mint, chives, basil, dill	1–2 small broccoli or cauliflower florets
1 tablespoon crème fraîche (or natural yogurt)	2–3 mangetout
For the crudités choose a colourful selection from:	2–3 baby sweetcorn
	25g (1oz) cucumber
½ small carrot	½ small parsnip
Small stick of celery	2–3 green beans or small runner beans

Wash then very finely chop the herbs and stir through the crème fraîche. When your child is more confident with finger food, most of the crudités can be eaten raw, but in the meantime wash and cut into small sticks or batons and steam for 2–3 minutes to soften. They can be eaten warm or chilled, covered and stored in the refrigerator for up to 12 hours.

Fruit Dips

You can dip fruit in breakfast purées, fruit purées, yogurts and fromage frais.

Makes 1 serving

Think rainbow colours when you select from:	½ dessert apple
	½ pear
½ small banana	3–4 grapes (seedless and halved)
25g (1oz) mango	
25g (1oz) papaya (paw paw)	½ kiwi fruit
½ peach	1–2 dried apricots or prunes (gently boiled until soft)
½ nectarine	

If the fruit is very ripe, simply cut into baby-sized batons, otherwise lightly steam until tender.

To sweeten natural yogurt , stir through a little apple juice, pineapple juice or cook and strain a few raspberries (removing the pips). See also Frozen Fruit Sticks on page 134.

Veggie treats

The following recipes are simple, easy introductions to proper meals. I've given you a range of tastes and textures to choose from and a couple of quick options (Bean Bites and My First Pizza) which will feed the baying masses in a moment.

Moroccan Couscous

Traditionally this is a combination of spicy fruit and vegetables with couscous (made from durum wheat). The recipe will also work well with quinoa instead of couscous. Ensure that you cook it until the grain is soft.
Makes 1–2 servings

100ml (3¹/₂fl oz) vegetable stock (see page 118) or water
25g (1oz) couscous
2 dried apricots
1 teaspoon olive oil
2 spring onions
25g (1oz) red pepper
1 dessertspoon peas (fresh or frozen)
1 garlic clove
50g (2oz) butternut squash purée (see page 64)
¹/₄ teaspoon finely chopped fresh coriander or small pinch of dried coriander
¹/₄ teaspoon cumin

Heat the stock in a medium saucepan. Rinse the couscous and chop the dried apricots and stir into the stock. Reduce the heat and gently simmer for 5–10 minutes to soak and soften.

Heat the oil in a non-stick frying pan. Finely chop all the other ingredients and sauté, adding the butternut squash purée towards the end to heat through as well as the herbs and cumin.

Mix in the couscous and apricots and serve as is or whizz slightly with a hand blender to suit your child.

If your child is over 12 months old and not allergic to nuts, try adding a few finely chopped cashews.

Cheesy Risotto

Traditionally risotto is made by gradually adding liquid to the rice, allowing the liquid to be soaked up by the rice before adding more. This is a simplified method – not traditional but practical.
Makes 1–2 servings

1 teaspoon olive oil
25g (1oz) leek
25g (1oz) courgette (also works well with broccoli, peas, green beans or fennel)
25g (1oz) red or yellow pepper
25g (1oz) butternut squash or red kuri
Large pinch of dried oregano
25g (1oz) wild, brown or risotto rice
125ml (4fl oz) vegetable stock (see page 118) or water
25g (1oz) hard cheese

Heat the oil in a medium saucepan. Wash and finely chop the leek, courgette, pepper and squash and add to the pan with the oregano. Stir well and gently cook for 2 minutes.

Rinse the rice and stir into the mix, coating the grains, then stir in the stock. Bring to the boil then reduce to a gentle simmer. Cover the pan and cook for 20 minutes until the rice is soft, stirring occasionally. Grate the cheese into the mix then melt in. Allow to cool to the right temperature for your baby and serve.

Tricolore Cold Pasta Salad

This cold salad is ideal for the child who wants to feed themselves and is able to chew as they will enjoy the mix of textures in finger-food-size pieces. For a less confident weaner use tiny soup pasta and cook, then whizz the other ingredients in a hand blender to make a fresh-tasting sauce.
Makes 1–2 servings

2 tablespoons pasta shapes
3 cherry tomatoes
25g (1oz) mangetout

25g (1oz) hard mild cheese, grated
Few fresh basil leaves (optional)

Cook the pasta following the instructions on the packet. Cut the cherry tomatoes in quarters and slice the mangetout into bite-size pieces. If your child is not yet able to chew confidently, steam the tomato and mangetout for 5 minutes until tender, otherwise leave raw.

Drain the pasta and rinse with cold water.

Combine all the ingredients and serve.

My First Pizza

Makes 4 mini pizzas

No-salt Dough (see page 126)
16 cherry tomatoes (4 per pizza)

40g (1¹/₂oz) mild hard cheese per pizza
Fresh basil leaves (optional)

Preheat the oven to 220°C/425°F/gas mark 7.

Shape the dough into 8cm (3¹/₄in) diameter discs and place on a lightly oiled baking tray.

Slice the cherry tomatoes into three and arrange on the dough discs. Grate the cheese and sprinkle on each. Bake for 15–20 minutes until the cheese begins to brown and the base is cooked but not hard.

Allow to cool and serve one with a sprinkle of chopped basil, if using. Freeze the others in individual bags.

Lentil, Fennel and Tofu

Makes 1–2 servings

125ml (4fl oz) vegetable stock (see page 118) or water
25g (1oz) dried red lentils
25g (1oz) potato
25g (1oz) fennel bulb
50g (2oz) firm tofu

25g (1oz) red pepper
25g (1oz) broccoli or green beans
¹/₄ teaspoon fresh parsley or chives

Bring the stock or water to a boil, reduce to a simmer and cover. Check the lentils for any stones or chaff and rinse thoroughly. Stir into the stock and continue to simmer for 15 minutes, adding more water if needed.

Wash, peel and chop the potato and add to the simmering lentils. Wash and shred the fennel, drain then cube the tofu, rinse and slice the pepper and broccoli and finely chop the herbs. Add to the stock, bring to the boil and return to a gentle simmer for 5–10 minutes until the potato and lentils are soft. Allow to cool and serve.

Fruity Bean Pilaf

Use tinned beans rather than cooking from dried, but choose beans that are tinned in water rather than sugared water or brine. Kidney beans, in particular, require very careful cooking from dried – if you do decide to go this route follow the on-pack instructions very carefully.

Makes 1 serving

40g (1½oz) mixed beans	15g (¾oz) sweetcorn
1 medium tomato (75g/3oz)	125ml (4fl oz) vegetable stock
1 dried apricot	(see page 118) or water
1 teaspoon sultanas	¼ teaspoon garam masala
25g (1oz) brown rice	
1 garlic clove	

Rinse and chop the beans, tomato, apricot and sultanas (if necessary).

Rinse and drain the rice and crush the garlic. Combine all the ingredients in a saucepan and bring to a boil, cover and reduce to a simmer. Cook for 20 minutes, stirring occasionally, until the rice is soft.

Allow to cool and serve.

Green Thai Tofu

This deliciously fragrant recipe includes creamed coconut. Coconut is not a high allergy risk, even though it is technically a nut, and it is extremely rare for anyone, even with a nut allergy, to react to coconut. Even so, as when introducing all new foods to your baby, start by making a small quantity early in the day to give you a chance to monitor any adverse reactions.

Makes 1 serving

1–2 teaspoons olive oil	2–3 button mushrooms
1 spring onion	3–4 green beans
1cm (½in) cube fresh ginger	75ml (3fl oz) vegetable stock
2cm (1in) lemongrass	(see page 118) or water
(optional)	½ teaspoon fresh coriander
40g (1½oz) potato	50g (2oz) firm tofu
25g (1oz) carrot	10g (½oz) creamed coconut
15g (¾oz) spinach or broccoli	or 1 tablespoon milk

Heat the oil in a non-stick frying pan. Slice the spring onion diagonally into strips, peel and grate the ginger and sauté with the lemongrass, if using.

Wash the other vegetables, peel and chop the potato and carrot into small cubes, tear the spinach or chop the broccoli and slice the mushrooms and beans. Add to the pan. Cook for 2 minutes to release the flavours but do not brown. Stir in the stock, bring to the boil and simmer. Finely chop the coriander and add to the pan. Cook for 5 minutes.

Drain the tofu and cut into small cubes and grate the creamed coconut, stir into the pan and simmer for another 8 minutes until the potato and carrot are soft.

Remember to remove the piece of lemongrass before serving. Allow to cool before serving.

Bean Bites

Many vegetarian dishes for this age tend to be wet stews and casseroles – not so great if your child loves finger food. Mini bean burgers can be eaten warm or cold.

Makes 8–12 bean bites

50g (2oz) tinned mixed beans
25g (1oz) sweet potato
15g (3/4oz) leek
2 teaspoons cornflour

1/4 teaspoon fresh herbs
  (optional)
1/4–1/2 egg, beaten
2–3 teaspoons olive oil

Rinse the beans and wash, peel and coarsely chop the sweet potato and leek. Put all the ingredients except the egg and olive oil into the chopping attachment of a hand blender and whizz until smooth (the mixture may be quite dry so you may not manage a completely smooth result).

Beat the egg and gradually add to the mix, using at least a quarter of the egg until the consistency resembles that of hummus.

Heat half the oil in a non-stick frying pan, then, using a teaspoon, drop blobs of the mixture into the pan, making sure that there's a little space between each one to prevent them sticking together. Cook for 4–5 minutes, drizzling in a little more oil as needed. Flip with a spatula, check the underside is golden, and cook for a further 4–5 minutes. Serve with steamed or raw crudités and dips.

Lentil Casserole

Makes 1–2 servings

200ml (7fl oz) vegetable stock
  (see page 118) or water
25g (1oz) dried red lentils
50g (2oz) squash (butternut
  or red kuri) or swede
25g (1oz) potato

25g (1oz) sweet potato
25g (1oz) parsnip
25g (1oz) leek
1 teaspoon fresh mixed herbs
  or 1/2 teaspoon dried mixed
  herbs

Heat the stock in a medium saucepan. Rinse the lentils, checking over for any small stones, and stir into the stock. Wash, peel and coarsely chop all the vegetables and stir into the stock, adding the herbs. Bring to the boil then either reduce to a gentle simmer, cover and cook for 30 minutes, stirring occasionally or, if you have the oven on, pour into a mini casserole dish, cover and bake at 150°C/300°F/gas mark 2 for 20–25 minutes.

Fruit and desserts

Shop-bought desserts can be a bit of a minefield of sugar and E numbers so I've included these healthy, natural options which are reasonably worthy but shouldn't send your child running to the hills in disgust.

Frozen Fruit (and Vegetable) Sticks

Gums can be very painful during these months with teething in full swing. Once your child is able to hold and chew a piece of fruit or a breadstick, this simple method will enable you to freeze hand-sized fruit sticks that will not only soothe sore gums, but also encourage your baby to eat more fruit and vegetables.

Choose from:
Apple
Peach
Nectarine

Plum
Carrot
Butternut squash
Sweet potato

Wash, peel and cut your chosen fruit and vegetables into baby-sized sticks.

Steam the vegetables for 6–8 minutes to soften. Leave to cool.

To prevent the sticks ending up as a large clump, lay the sticks on a baking tray (checking first that it will fit in your freezer), ensuring there is space between each one. Freeze for 1 hour then transfer into small freezer bags. When required allow the sticks to warm up a little – if you give them to your child straight from the freezer they can be too cold and freeze burn (if in doubt check one yourself first).

Hint Older children will love these too, especially in summer when you can include berries. Serve on their own or with yogurt.

Apple Cinnamon Crumble Pot

Little ovenproof ramekin dishes are perfect for making these individual crumble pots. See the Oaty Crumble recipe on page 50 for ideas on how to spice it up and add ingredients for an adult version.
Makes 1 serving

½ dessert apple or 3–4 cubes apple purée (see page 70)
1 teaspoon sultanas (chopped if large)

Pinch of cinnamon
1 dessertspoon oats
15g (¾oz) butter (very cold)

Preheat the oven to 200°C/400°F/gas mark 6.

Wash, peel and chop the apple and cook with a little water in a small saucepan (or melt the frozen purée). Stir in the sultanas and cinnamon and simmer for 3–4 minutes. Pour into the ramekin.

Put the oats in the chopping bowl of a hand blender and grate in the butter. Whizz until they resemble breadcrumbs and sprinkle onto the apple mixture. Bake for 15 minutes until slightly golden. Leave to cool a little before serving.

This recipe works well with most other fruit, although if made with banana it will not freeze well.

Real Fruit Jelly

Most shop-bought jelly cubes are high in artificial colours and flavours, but it is surprisingly easy to make your own fruit jellies with either gelatine or the vegetarian alternative, agar agar. Some fruits are too acidic and won't set however hard you try, for example kiwi fruit, and some require cooking first (see below) because they contain an enzyme that will prevent them from setting. Choose powdered gelatine or agar agar if you can, otherwise follow the packet instructions to dissolve.

Makes 2 servings

2 heaped teaspoons powdered gelatine or agar agar
500ml (18fl oz) juice made up of one or more of the following:
Apple
Pear
Grape
Red- or blackcurrant
Blackberry
Raspberry

The following are brought to a boil for 5 minutes before adding the gelatine or agar agar:
Pineapple
Mango
Papaya
Peach
Nectarine

If making the juices yourself, wash the fruit and bring to the boil in a little water until soft then strain to remove skins and pips etc. Make up to 500ml (18fl oz) by adding extra apple juice for sweetness.

Put the juice in a clean saucepan, bring to the boil and simmer, then sprinkle in the gelatine or agar agar, stirring continuously until fully dissolved.

Put some cold water on to a saucer and drip a couple of drops of the mix on to the water to check it is strong enough to set – it should form a jelly blob. If not, sprinkle in a little more gelatine or agar agar and repeat. If it goes very thick add a little more apple juice.

Pour into jelly moulds, cool and refrigerate until set (takes about 3 hours).

Christmas dinner treats

Christmas is the time of a few extra drinks, a few extra puds and a few sneaky kisses under the mistletoe and your child will want to be part of festive activities as they feed on your anticipation of the upcoming event. While overindulging them isn't wise and buying presents is a bit pointless as the wrapping paper will be far more enticing than the gift itself, there is a way to treat your child. Grab the high chair, make them the centre of attention at the table and serve these treats at the same time as the main meal. They'll just love being part of the big dinner extravaganza!

Turkey Christmas Dinner

Makes 1 serving

50g (2oz) turkey breast
25g (1oz) carrot
25g (1oz) parsnip
25g (1oz) potato or sweet
  potato

25g (1oz) leek
25g (1oz) broccoli or
  1 Brussels sprout
2–3 fresh sage leaves or pinch
  of dried sage

Rinse the turkey breast and chop into ½–1cm (¼–½in) cubes. Steam the turkey and meanwhile wash and peel the vegetables and chop into ½–1cm (¼–½in) cubes. Add the vegetables with the sage to the turkey and steam for a further 5 minutes until the turkey is thoroughly cooked and the vegetables are soft (the turkey should be steamed for 10–12 minutes in total).

    Serve as is to a confident independent weaner with the collected steamer stock, or whizz with a hand blender to a chunky purée.

My First Christmas Pudding

Traditional Christmas pudding is too rich (and alcoholic!) to give to a young child – here's a simplified version. It is delicious as it is or serve with a swirl of natural yogurt.

Makes 1 serving

2 prunes (stones removed)
2–3 dried apricots (sulphur-
  free, stones removed)
1 teaspoon sultanas or raisins
40g (1½oz) apple

25g (1oz) carrot
1 dessertspoon oats
Large pinch of mixed spice,
  e.g. cinnamon, ginger
1 tablespoon whole milk

Roughly chop the prunes and apricots, removing any bits of stone. Put in a saucepan with the sultanas or raisins and enough water to cover them and bring to the boil.

    Wash, peel and grate the apple and the carrot and add to the dried fruit. Simmer for 1 minute. Stir in the oats and spices with the milk and a little extra water if needed. Cover, bring back to the boil and simmer for 8–10 minutes, stirring occasionally.

From 9 months: Independent Weaning

Milk is still important; however, by this stage guidelines recommend no more than 500–600ml (18fl oz–1 pint) per day, although the planner does not specify how this should be spread across the day – vary to suit your child.

Fruit and vegetables are important. Keep a lidded plastic container in the fridge with a selection of fruit and vegetable sticks and dried fruit as handy snacks between meals – the coolness will also soothe sore gums.

Your baby will enjoy learning to feed themselves, but never leave a baby alone with cutlery or finger foods.

Remember to include a drink of water with mealtimes.

	Wake-up	Breakfast	Lunch	Mid-afternoon	Dinner	Supper	Bedtime (optional)
Day 1	Breast milk or formula milk	No-gluten Muesli (see p85) with **Fruit Dips** (see p128)	**Chicken Curry** (see p122) with broccoli florets or green beans **Peach, Plum and Vanilla** (see p91)	Breast milk or formula milk	**Broccoli and Peas with Cheese** (see p107) **Banana and Prune Purée** (see p84)	Breast milk or formula milk	Breast milk or formula milk *
Day 2	Breast milk or formula milk	**Plum and Porridge Pancakes** (see p117)	**Fish Creole** (see p120) with rice or noodles **Pear, Raisin and Sultana Purée** (see p93)	Breast milk or formula milk	**No-salt Breadsticks** (see p126) with **Dips** (see p128) Yogurt or fromage frais	Breast milk or formula milk	Breast milk or formula milk *
Day 3	Breast milk or formula milk	**Beginner's Porridge** (see p84) with **Fruit Dips** (see p128)	**Mini Meatballs** in **Meatball Sauce** (see p124–5) with broccoli florets Fresh fruit pieces	Breast milk or formula milk	**Cheesy Risotto** (see p129) **Apple and Mango Purée** (see p96)	Breast milk or formula milk	Breast milk or formula milk *
Day 4	Breast milk or formula milk	**French Toast** (see p116)	**Green Thai Tofu** (see p132) **Strawberry and Banana Mash** (see p93)	Breast milk or formula milk	**My First Pizza** (see p131) **Real Fruit Jelly** (see p135)	Breast milk or formula milk	Breast milk or formula milk *
Day 5	Breast milk or formula milk	No-gluten Muesli (see p85) with **Fruit Dips** (see p128)	**Bean Bites** (p133 or p119, p123) with **Eggy Mash** (see p107) **Fruit Dips** (see p128)	Breast milk or formula milk	**Tricolore Cold Pasta Salad** (see p131) **Mango with Blackberry Ripple** (see p95)	Breast milk or formula milk	Breast milk or formula milk *
Day 6	Breast milk or formula milk	**Cheese Dreams** (see p117)	**Grandma Daisy's Casserole** (see p122) Fresh fruit pieces	Breast milk or formula milk	**Herby Crème Fraîche with Crudités** (see p128) **Apple Cinnamon Crumble Pot** (see p134)	Breast milk or formula milk	Breast milk or formula milk *
Day 7	Breast milk or formula milk	**Beginner's Porridge** (see p84) with **Fruit Dips** (see p128)	**Fisherman's Pie** (see p119) Yogurt or fromage frais	Breast milk or formula milk	**Lentil, Fennel and Tofu** (see p131) **Nectarine and Dried Apricot Purée** (see p92)	Breast milk or formula milk	Breast milk or formula milk *

* Optional although many babies find it a comforting part of their bedtime routine.

Stage four:
Towards adult food

This section provides healthy, easy-to-prepare, toddler meals as well as tips on introducing difficult vegetables (including a recipe on how to make Cabbage Ice Cream!).

The fourth stage

This section includes more meal ideas but also deals with areas where you may be struggling to get your child to eat. Stage 4 meals are for 12 months and on, but remember to include stage 3 meals and increase the portions.

Toddler meals

As a toddler's tastebuds go on the magical mystery tour of discovery, you'll find their choices will be as wide and varied as Rod Stewart's back catalogue. Some children don't like to see what they're eating while others need to have every food displayed on their plate. Some children will like fantasy foods (just rename a dish 'Bob the Builder's porridge'), while others simply want to get stuck in. Some children will like three big sit-down meals with a few snacks in between, while others are natural-born grazers.

Struggling with food – the neophobic response

You may find that your child is neophobic, but this doesn't mean a trip to the doctor, just an in-built fear of new foods and new things in general. Essentially it's a survival technique and understanding it will help to explain why your child can seemingly switch from a happy-go-lucky 'I'll taste anything' babe to an 'If you think I'm eating that you're bonkers' toddler. The neophobic response kicks in at around the age your child learns to crawl and walk and is beginning to explore away from the watchful eyes of adults. Previously your child will have happily put anything into their mouths. Now, however, they will become increasingly sceptical and extremely cautious when they encounter foods they don't recognise, either flatly refusing or spitting out alien substances. One way to introduce new foods is to mix them in with foods you know they like. It's important not to give up as a more varied diet at this stage should mean your child is less picky later.

Brain food

Children's food intake, at this age, is like a yo-yo. Your child might eat a continent-sized lunch, but an itsy-bitsy-teeny-weeny dinner. Just go with the flow. As Elizabeth Morse says in *My Child Won't Eat*, 'If a child grew at the same rate as in the first year, they would be 29 metres long and weigh 200 tonnes by the age of ten.' A toddler's appetite does lose momentum, but they will need a steady stream of food as their brain is dissecting and processing information. At this age, it's not surprising that two-thirds of their food is used by the brain. To keep their blood sugar up, small people need to eat and drink every two to three hours – even if it's just a snack.

A rough guide to a 2-year-old's daily intake

You don't need a meal planner for this stage, but here is a checklist so that you can ensure your child is getting a good mix of the food groups below.

3–4 servings of fruit and veg

(an apple, a peach, broccoli florets, lettuce and tomatoes)

3–5 servings of carbohydrate

(a slice of bread, a serving of potatoes, a bowl of pasta)

3 servings of dairy food

(a fromage frais, yogurt, slices of cheese, a glass of warm milk)

1 serving of animal protein or
2 servings of vegetable protein

(1 egg, 1 peanut butter sandwich, a serving of fish, chicken or beef, tofu, pulses, nuts)

Avoiding food fights

Eating is one of life's great pleasures so try to keep mealtimes breezy and fun. The minute you start force-feeding, bribing or cajoling your child with food, mealtimes can become a power struggle. Though a child may learn that, 'Yuck, I don't like it' can get them yummier alternatives, the challenge for you is to find out whether they are not eating simply because they're not feeling too good, they're teething, they don't like the taste or texture of the food, or because there are more exciting things to do.

Here are some ways to avoid food stand-offs

One of the golden rules of getting your baby to eat is to eat with them

If you've eaten alone in a restaurant you'll know it can be a disconcerting experience, so don't be surprised if your baby struggles to eat under your beady eye. If your baby sees you tucking in too, however, they'll be inspired to do the same.

Vary the venue. If you've reached a stand-off, simply transport them to somewhere different, like a picnic rug on the living-room floor or an outdoor space if you've got one.

It's perfectly normal for your baby to love a food one week and loathe it the next

Just take it away and try it again later.

Ensure that the food is neither too hot nor too cold. Most babies love warm food as it's reminiscent of breast milk and easy to swallow. However, try to present them with slight variations in temperature so you don't end up with a fussy toddler who won't eat cold food.

It's not unusual for an independent weaner to get annoyed when you try to feed them, particularly rejecting smooth purées in favour of foods they find easier to feed themselves with. Conversely don't be surprised if on off-days they are more than happy to be mummy's or daddy's little baby again and relish the comfort of being spoon-fed.

Avoid overloading your baby's plate as too much food can seem overwhelming

Instead, give your baby a small amount and give them loads of praise when it's gone down the hatch before spooning out more (for example, 'Oh – you are a great eater. I wonder if you can eat some more').

Note Babies of this age are getting smarter and may realise that if they fuss enough and refuse to eat their main course they'll get an alternative, like yogurt or biscuits. Keep desserts as an occasional treat. If they do get fussy, just remove the plate and don't offer anything else except maybe a piece of fruit or a slice of cheese until the next meal by which time they should be very hungry. While a child may assert their independence, they will never starve themselves.

Breakfast to go

Breakfast can be a social time, even if it is a bit dine and dash. If you're a working parent most days you won't have time to create a fresh breakfast from scratch so a store cupboard full of home-made mueslis and bread variations is quick and easy. Here is a handful of recipes (don't forget the recipes in the earlier sections too) that take a few minutes to rustle up and provide your child with a morning's worth of good nutrition. Some of these ideas make excellent desserts or snacks too.

Banana Toast with Yogurt

Cooking in butter, for a minute, caramelises the banana into a sticky delight. For this recipe you could also use raisin or fruit bread, pannetone or just a plain wholemeal muffin.
Makes 1 serving

1 tablespoon unsalted butter
1 ripe banana
2 tablespoons maple syrup
Pinch of cinnamon

Sprinkling of finely chopped toasted almonds (if not allergic)
1 slice of raisin or fruit bread
Dollop of yogurt

Melt the butter in a non-stick frying pan. Peel and diagonally slice the banana and fry for a minute or two. Add the maple syrup, a pinch of cinnamon and mix in the almonds, if using.

Toast and butter the bread and cut into triangles or wedges. Spoon on the banana mix and serve with yogurt and a dusting of cinnamon.

Groovy Granola

Make a big batch of this on a Sunday (you may want to double the recipe) and store in an airtight container. Involve your child in selecting what they want in their granola – they could name it too. This also makes a good topping for apple crumble or a healthy granola bar.
Makes 2–3 servings

1 tablespoon sunflower seeds
1 tablespoon pumpkin seeds
1 dessertspoon linseeds (flax seeds)
50g (2oz) hazelnuts (omit if there is a nut allergy)

110g (4oz) rolled oats
2 tablespoons sunflower oil
2 tablespoons organic honey
50g (2oz) raisins or sultanas

Preheat the oven to 180°C/350°F/gas mark 4.

Grind up all the seeds (and nuts if using) roughly in a blender and combine with the oats in a baking tray.

Melt the sunflower oil and honey together in a saucepan and pour this mixture into the baking tray, ensuring all the oat mixture gets a good coating.

Bake for about 30 minutes, stirring occasionally, until the mixture is golden. Remove from the oven and mix in the raisins or sultanas. Store in an airtight container. Serve with milk or yogurt and fresh fruit.

Eggs: Scrambled or Bang Bang!

It's quick, it's nutritious, it's scramblers with hot, unsalted-buttered toast. Alternatively go for Bang Bang Eggs aka boiled egg – which sounds more fun and will remind them that they get to crack the top with a spoon. Serve with toast soldiers. Eggs need to be hard boiled for babies and young children.
Makes 1 serving

1 egg   1 tablespoon whole milk
½ teaspoon olive oil

Heat a small saucepan on the stove. Beat together all the ingredients in a bowl, then pour into the pan. Stir continuously until the mix is just moist (but not dry). Serve on toast or rolled in a fresh soft tortilla.

For extra nutrition and variety, you can add a number of ingredients into the mix, like grated cheese, flaked tuna fish (tinned in oil or water, not brine), tomatoes, or finely chopped peppers.

If you want Bang Bang Eggs, hardboil the egg for 8–10 minutes.

Purple Porridge

Hard to compete with the free gizmos and promotions of the commercial stuff – and some are great for kids, especially served with fresh fruit for sweetness and variety, but others are high in refined sugar, which will give your child a quick burst of energy that'll make them crash and burn.

Compared to packaged cereals, home-made porridge may seem dull, dull, dull, so here's a recipe that gets away from the usual brown mush – and is a hit with kids and adults alike. And yes, it really is bright purple!
Makes 1 serving

25g (1oz) porridge or rolled   50g (1oz) fresh or frozen
  oats   summer fruits
100ml (3½fl oz) milk   (blackcurrants, redcurrants,
1 teaspoon sunflower seeds   cherries, raspberries,
  (whole or ground)   strawberries, blackberries)
1 teaspoon pumpkin seeds   1 teaspoon honey
  (whole or ground)

Combine all the ingredients in a medium saucepan and bring to the boil. Reduce the heat and simmer for 5–8 minutes, until the oats are soft, and serve as is or with yogurt.

To freeze your own summer fruits, remove all stalks and stones, rinse in a colander and drain. Spread the fruits on a large baking tray and freeze for 1–2 hours. Bag up into small freezer bags, date and label. If you bag up soft fruits without pre-freezing you will end up with a solid clump; this method helps to keep them loose.

Vegetables: the art of disguise

This can be a tricky age when it comes to eating vegetables and I often hear parents lamenting that their children won't eat greens. If your child is a late starter, I recommend the art of disguise as a short-term fix, but in the long term you'll need to get them acquainted. One way is to offer your child a little raw or cooked veg with each meal, so they can feel, see and smell them. While you're hiding vegetables in, under or around foods that you know your child will eat, also put out new foods to introduce them to. Instead of expecting them to try foods out of the blue, present the food a dozen times over a period of weeks. Just as curiosity got the cat, your tot will eventually try them.

Children are notoriously picky. For 2-year-olds their version of a gastronomic delight is buttered toast, while broccoli can be an alien life form. Get your toddler to help you prepare the food. They can wash vegetables, add chopped vegetables to dishes, stir and play 'tester' – it all helps to break down the barriers.

Many children are averse to fresh produce being introduced at this stage, particularly if they have been weaned on commercial babyfood, which is generally monotextured and bland. If this is the case, you may need to re-wean your toddler. Take them back a step to more mashed foods, then try finely diced foods and finally whole foods. Children are also more likely to accept – and taste – new foods that are similar to foods they know. If, for example, they like peaches, nectarines aren't a big deviation. Or, if they like a meat burger, they'll like a chicken burger or a veggie burger.

Another way is to serve their favourite dish with a few variations (scrambled eggs with smoked salmon, mushrooms, cheese). And, of course, anything can be disguised when it's squashed between two bits of bread or rolled up in a tortilla.

Secret Agent Sauce aka Hidden Vegetable Sauce

Makes 2–4 servings

FOR THE BASIC SAUCE
15g (¾oz) red onion
1 teaspoon olive oil
25g (1oz) carrot
25g (1oz) sweet potato
15g (¾oz) fresh beetroot or
  1 cube beetroot purée (see
  page 66)
2–3 tablespoons water
25g (1oz) red pepper

1 small ripe tomato (75g/3oz)
25g (1oz) broccoli
25g (1oz) courgette
25g (1oz) spinach
3–4 button mushrooms
1 garlic clove
1–2 tablespoons whole milk
1 teaspoon Worcester sauce
Freshly ground black pepper

Finely chop the onion and gently cook with the olive oil in a small saucepan. Wash, peel and finely chop the carrot and sweet potato (if using fresh beetroot, finely peel, chop and add here) and add to the onion, cook for a further 3 minutes then add the water and gently simmer.

Wash and finely chop the red pepper, tomato, broccoli, courgette, spinach, mushrooms and garlic and add with the milk. Simmer for a further 4 minutes. If using beetroot purée, stir through a little at a time to colour the sauce to the desired red.

Whizz with a hand blender to the appropriate texture for your child. Season with Worcester sauce and pepper to taste.

Quick sauce method: if you have a younger child who is weaning or about to and you have frozen cubes of purée, simply sweat the onion with the olive oil and add in a cube of the various purées (our stage 1 pots can also be used for extra convenience). Heat until defrosted. Wash and finely chop the tomato and red pepper and stir in with the milk (and, if needed, additional water). Blend as before.

Serve on pasta, adding crème fraîche, mascarpone cheese or grated hard cheese to make it creamy and to add protein, or use instead of ketchup.

Mighty Meaty Pasta Sauce

A meat pasta sauce hides a multitude of vegetable sins, but made this way it also provides iron coupled with vitamin-rich vegetables. Just as with the Secret Agent Sauce, feel free to chop and change the hidden vegetables to what's in season or whatever you know you'll get away with hiding – such as spinach in place of peas.

Makes 1 serving

1 teaspoon olive oil
½ medium onion (50g/2oz)
1 garlic clove
50–75g (2–3oz) lean mince
  (beef, lamb, chicken, turkey)
¼ red pepper
3–4 button mushrooms
1 dessertspoon fresh or
  frozen peas
25g (1oz) carrot (or 1 cube
  carrot purée, see page 60)

25g (1oz) sweet potato (or
  1 cube sweet potato purée,
  see page 60)
1 medium tomato (or 1 tinned
  plum tomato)
½ teaspoon tomato purée
1 tablespoon water or stock
  (see page 118)
¼ teaspoon oregano
1 tablespoon fresh parsley

Heat the oil in a non-stick frying pan. Dice, peel and finely chop the onion and crush the garlic and gently cook in the oil until the onion starts to soften. Increase the heat slightly, add the mince and keep stirring until the mince is cooked and just begins to brown, then reduce the heat to low.

Wash, peel and finely chop the other vegetables and add to the mix (grate the carrot and sweet potato to speed up cooking time along with the remaining ingredients). Gently simmer until all the vegetables are soft then whizz with a hand blender to a fairly smooth sauce.

Serve over a bed of spaghetti, on top of freshly cooked mash or baked potatoes topped with cheese, or allow to cool and freeze until needed.

Vegetable ice creams

You probably think I'm having a laugh if I imagine any of you are going near these. But if I told you, or more importantly a child who doesn't like vegetables, that I had some delicious purple ice cream or an orange frozen yogurt you wouldn't be surprised to find children are quite willing to try my Frankenstein creations. And, just to encourage you, not one of the groups of parents I tried these on was able to tell me what was in Cabbage or Brussels Sprout Ice Cream. So don't be scared and remember you're not creating a monster but a masterpiece.

Frozen Yogurt

Parsnip and Pear Frozen Yogurt or White Ice Cream

150g (5oz) parsnip	250g (9oz) whole natural
150g (5oz) very ripe pear	yogurt

Wash and peel the parsnip, removing the tough centre core and grate or very finely chop. Wash, peel, core and grate the pear. Put the parsnip and the pear in a saucepan with just enough boiling water to cover, reduce the heat and simmer for 10–15 minutes until the largest piece of parsnip is soft.

Whizz in the chopping attachment of a hand blender until   smooth, pour into a container and cover. Set aside to cool then chill in the refrigerator.

Stir 250g (9oz) of the parsnip and pear purée into the yogurt. Churn in the ice-cream maker until thick then scoop individual portions into lidded, freezer-proof containers. Freeze until required.

Note All recipes require an ice-cream maker (see manufacturer's instructions for use).
Home-made ice cream can be stored for up to 3 months in a standard domestic freezer.

Carrot and Orange Frozen Yogurt or Orange Ice Cream

If your child likes the sharpness of citrus, replace a little of the orange juice with fresh lemon juice to make it super zingy.

150g (5oz) carrot	250g (9oz) whole natural
200ml (7fl oz) freshly	yogurt
squeezed orange juice	

Wash and peel the carrots and grate or very finely chop. Stir the carrot into the orange juice and bring to the boil in a medium saucepan. Reduce the heat and simmer for 10–15 minutes until the largest piece of carrot is soft and the juice has reduced in volume by about one-third.

Whizz in the chopping attachment of a hand blender until smooth, pour into a container and cover. Set aside to cool then chill in the refrigerator.

Stir 250g (9oz) of the carrot and orange purée into the yogurt. Churn in the ice-cream maker until thick, then scoop individual portions into lidded, freezer-proof containers. Freeze until required.

Ice Creams

Minty Pea Ice Cream

1–4 sprigs of fresh mint
250g (9oz) frozen peas

150ml (¼ pint) whipping cream
100ml (3½fl oz) whole milk

Wash the mint and tear or coarsely chop (vary the quantity to suit your child).

Bring to the boil just enough water to cover the mint and peas, add, then reduce to a simmer for 10 minutes until the peas are very soft. Whizz in the chopping attachment of a hand blender, adding the water the peas were cooked in to make a glossy, smooth purée.

Pour into a container and cover. Set aside to cool then chill in the refrigerator. Stir 250g (9oz) of the minty pea purée into the cream and milk. Churn in the ice-cream maker until thick, then scoop individual portions into lidded, freezer-proof containers. Freeze until required.

Purple or Creamy Green Ice Cream

Red cabbage gives this a lovely natural purple colour and the apple and sultanas soften the bitterness. Vary the amount of cinnamon to suit your child. If your child takes to this why not get ambitious and try Brussels sprouts?

75g (3oz) red cabbage or
  8 Brussels sprouts
60g (2½oz) dessert apple
25g (1oz) sultanas

15g (¾oz) butter
½ teaspoon cinnamon
150ml (¼ pint) whipping cream
100ml (3½fl oz) whole milk

Wash and finely shred the cabbage. Wash, peel, core and grate the apple and rinse the sultanas. Melt the butter in a medium saucepan, reduce the heat then stir in the cabbage, apple, sultanas and cinnamon. Cook for 2–3 minutes, stirring frequently to avoid burning. Add 2–4 tablespoons of water, bring to a boil, then immediately reduce to a gentle simmer for 10 minutes. Check the largest piece of cabbage is soft.

Whizz in the chopping attachment of a hand blender to make a glossy, very smooth purée.

Pour into a container and cover. Set aside to cool then chill in the refrigerator. Stir the cabbage purée into the cream and milk. Churn in the ice-cream maker until thick, then scoop individual portions into lidded, freezer-proof containers. Freeze until required.

Green Ice Cream

This recipe is the most savoury tasting of these recipes – think of a light frozen herb butter rather than an ice cream. Serve on its own or with hot grilled meat, poultry or fish and mashed potato. It will melt to give a savoury creamy sauce.

150g (5oz) broccoli
50g (2oz) leeks
4–5 basil leaves

125ml (4fl oz) whole milk
1 egg yolk
150ml (¼ pint) whipping cream

Wash and trim the stalks of the broccoli and leeks, then finely chop. Rinse the basil leaves. Bring 100ml (3½fl oz) of the milk to the boil then add the broccoli, leek and basil. Return to the boil, then simmer for 10–12 minutes until the largest piece is soft. Push the mix through a sieve, reserving the cooking milk, and whizz the veg in the chopping attachment of a hand blender to make a glossy, very smooth purée, adding a little of the boiled milk as needed.

Beat the egg yolk with the remaining 25ml (½fl oz) milk then pour into the saucepan with the rest of the boiled milk. Cook for 4–5 minutes over a gentle heat, stirring continuously until it thickens slightly but don't let it boil as this will cause the mix to separate (if your child has an egg allergy the recipe will work without the egg custard). Put the puréed vegetable mix, milk and egg in lidded containers and set aside to cool, then chill in the refrigerator.

Combine 200g (7oz) of the broccoli purée with the egg custard and cream. Churn in the ice-cream maker until thick, then scoop individual portions into lidded, freezer-proof containers. Freeze until required.

Jazz 'em up

If you are having trouble getting your little one to eat vegetables and your cunning disguises are as much use as a newspaper with eyeholes cut out, then go the other way and make the vegetables the exciting part of their meal. If all else fails get them to help you wash, peel and chop the vegetables because, as you know, it's harder to turn your nose up at something when you know the amount of effort that's been put in.

Roast Them All

The roast potato is familiar to all of us, but why stop there? This recipe is a quick and easy way to prepare lots of vegetables at once – the slow roast gives you the time to do other things while filling the kitchen with delicious aromas.
Makes 1–4 servings (depending on how many vegetables you prepare)

3–4 tablespoons olive oil
2 garlic cloves crushed
 (optional)
2 sprigs of fresh rosemary
 (optional)

A selection of the following:
1 carrot
50g (2oz) pumpkin/squash
 (e.g. butternut squash or red
 kuri)

1 medium potato
1 sweet potato
1 parsnip
1 beetroot
1–2 baby leeks
2–3 shallots
1/2 red or green pepper
50g (2oz) yam

Preheat the oven to 180°C/350°F /gas mark 4.

Heat the olive oil in a large roasting tin with the garlic and rosemary, if using.

Wash, peel and chop the selection of vegetables roughly into 2cm (3/4 in) cubes.

When the oven is up to temperature, toss the medley of vegetables in the oil and roast for 30–40 minutes, turning the veg a couple of times. Cook until crispy and browning on the outside, soft on the inside. Once cooked simply reduce the heat to 140°C/275°F/gas mark 1 and cook slowly for up to 40 minutes to enhance the flavour.

Tempura Vegetables

Tempura vegetables are fried, so they should not be eaten at every meal, but they make a quick, special treat when friends are visiting or if you are trying to get a child's interest back into the world of vegetables. Just like Revels, part of the fun of tempura is not knowing what's inside – the cheese chunks will be a gooey surprise.

Makes 2 servings (not suitable for freezing)

A selection of the following:	10g (1/2oz) cornflour
1/2 carrot	1/2 teaspoon olive oil
4 sugarsnap peas	1 tablespoon water
4 button mushrooms	1 egg white (for an idea of
2 baby sweetcorn	what to do with the yolk see
4 small florets broccoli	Cheesy Footballs recipe,
1/2 courgette	page 162)
4 chunks of pineapple	
4 chunks of cheese	
200ml (7fl oz) sunflower oil	

Prepare the vegetables. Thinly slice the carrot and halve the sugarsnap peas, mushrooms and baby sweetcorn. Cut the courgette into chunks.

Fill a wok or deep frying pan 3–4cm (1¼–1½in) deep with oil (note: this recipe does not work with olive oil because olive oil will not get hot enough).

Mix the cornflour with the olive oil and water. Beat the egg white until stiff and fold into the cornflour mix. Pour the chopped ingredients into the fluffy batter.

Heat the oil and deep fry the chunks in batches, 4–5 at a time. The batter will swell and crispen. Turn once to make sure the tempura is golden on each side and use a slotted spoon to remove. Lay the pieces on a couple of sheets of kitchen paper to soak up the excess oil. Repeat until finished.

Serve immediately.

Stir Fry

This oriental method of cooking is often a hit with kids as it combines the crunch of raw food with the comfort of hot food. Typically sesame or groundnut oils are used; however both are known to be a higher allergy risk, so if in any doubt stick to olive oil (as this recipe suggests).

Makes 1–2 servings

Select a colourful combination from the following:	25g (1oz) beansprouts or alfalfa
1/2 carrot	25g (1oz) water chestnuts (tinned)
1/2 stick of celery	25g (1oz) bamboo shoots (tinned)
1/2 courgette	25g (1oz) pak choi
2 spring onions	
2–3 mushrooms	1–2 tablespoons olive oil
4–5 mangetout	1 garlic clove, crushed (optional)
4–5 green beans	1 tablespoon low-salt soy sauce
25g (1oz) spinach leaves	Juice of 1/4 lime
25g (1oz) cabbage	
2–3 baby sweetcorn	
3–4 small broccoli florets	
1/4 red, green or yellow pepper	

Wash, peel and slice your selection of ingredients into bite-sized pieces.

Heat the oil in a non-stick wok (or large non-stick frying pan) with the crushed garlic, if using. Put the chopped ingredients into the pan and stir frequently to coat and heat through. Some children like the taste of the slightly browned bits so vary the cooking time to suit your child. Toss in the soy and lime juice, then serve.

Keeping it simple

While some children like mixed-up food, others like to see what they're eating. They like their food boring and safe. Serving food in compartments means they'll get an array of appetising foods from which they can pick 'n' mix. If you're using saucepans, you could go loopy, so try using a steamer with dividing walls, which will help you cook small amounts separated at the same time, including fish, meat and rice. Raw food can be harder to digest so another option is to part-steam the veg then serve warm or cold.

Simple Steamers

100g (3½oz) chicken fillet   **1 tablespoon sweetcorn**
50g (2oz) broccoli   **1 small carrot**

Cut the chicken into goujons. Wash, then cut or break the broccoli into small florets, slice off the sweetcorn from a cob (or use unsweetened sweetcorn tinned in water not brine). Wash, peel and slice the carrot into fine sticks.

Using the dividers, steam the ingredients separately and serve on a plate with divisions or a large plate with plenty of space in between.

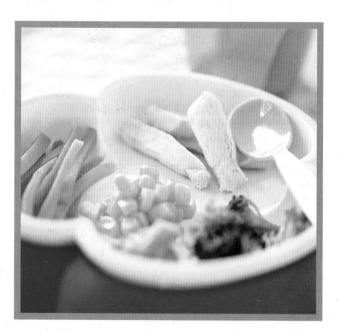

Veggie Pick 'n' Mix

Most adults like a big bowl of salad with everything mixed but some children find this too messy. Try keeping all the vegetables separate so your child can pick 'n' mix. If one particular vegetable is left, you can work out why your child doesn't like mixed salad.

Children may also take to separated salads as the crunch of some foods like cabbage can make them more appealing raw than cooked.

Remember to select a variety of colours as a quick way to balance nutrition.

Select a colourful combination from the following:
Red and yellow peppers
Cabbage
Cherry tomatoes
Sweet potato
Carrot
Cauliflower
Mangetout
Celery
Cucumber
Avocado

Making mealtime a learning time

Food and eating can become boring compared to toys, videos and TV programmes. Try looking at mealtimes as a learning time. Clear the table of toys and distractions and set it for both of you. Turn off the TV or radio and treat it as a special 'us' time.

Rather than creating artistic masterpieces think creatively about themes relating to what they're into at the moment and what they're learning about at playgroup, on TV or in their favourite book. Think of eating as part of the learning rather than the main focus of mealtime. Here are a few ideas to get you started.

Learning to count

OK, this is easy peasy. You could line the food up like a multi-coloured abacus (1 slice of courgette, 2 slices of carrot, 3 pieces of yellow pepper, 4 cherry tomatoes, 5 grapes). Or line up 1 home-made chicken/fish/veggie goujon, 2 boiled potatoes, 3 baby carrots, 4 string beans. They can subtract them by eating them. And then how many are left?

Colours

On a large plate, place a selection of different-coloured foods and ask, 'What colour are the peas?' If they get it right, they can eat them and so on.

Face-off

Almost any meal can be turned into a face. This is quick and easy to do. For example, with a salad, just halve 2 yellow cherry tomatoes for eyes, use raisins as eyeballs, add a nose with a sausage; use a wedge of red pepper for a mouth and sliced hard-boiled-egg moon shapes for ears. Create hair from cooked pasta in pesto or mashed potato. It's even easier with fruit. Try a couple of grapes for eyes, half a banana for a nose, an apple wedge for a mouth, raisins for the hair and a couple of mandarin wedges for the ears.

Clock-face

Place peas or sliced cooked or raw carrots (or courgettes, potatoes or whatever you like) around the rim of a plate. Make the clock hands from carrots, cheese, red or green pepper or celery cut lengthways. Create the 'centrepiece' from a home-made burger, egg or a pile of tuna, ham or other source of protein. Then your child can eat every 'number' the hands points to!

Giant's dinner or witch's playground

This one just involves creating a 'landscape' from food. For example, make a forest from broccoli 'trees', towers of carrots (just stand them on end), mountains of mash, boulder cherry tomatoes... you've got it in one.

Healthy fast food

Fast food is not necessarily junk food. No doubt you'll have decided you will never feed your child burgers or chicken nuggets. Don't do it. Before you set a hard rod for your back, don't forget that banning foods is a surefire way to make them more attractive to a belligerent toddler. Right now, 'junk foods' are a hot potato in the food industry, but the truth is snacks and food in a flash can be healthy. Yes, even burgers and chicken nuggets.

DIY Burgers (Classic, Salmon and Veg)

A chameleon of a recipe: fish, meat or poultry, smooth or chunky to suit your child's fancy. Keep it simple with the basic recipe or select from the optional extras to add in a few hidden veggies.

Makes 10 small burgers

BASIC RECIPE

310g (11oz) salmon or trout fillet, skinned and chopped into ½cm (¼in) cubes
or
310g (11oz) beef, lamb, pork, turkey or chicken mince or chopped into ½cm (¼in) cubes
½ medium onion
50g (2oz) oats
1 medium egg
1 tablespoon flour (corn or plain wheat)
1 tablespoon olive oil

OPTIONAL EXTRAS

1 dessertspoon finely chopped, fresh, herbs (e.g. coriander, tarragon, basil, mint, oregano or parsley)
Pinch of mild spice, e.g. paprika, cumin, turmeric
1 tablespoon shredded spinach
1 garlic clove, crushed
1 dessertspoon chopped red or yellow pepper
1 tablespoon finely chopped mushrooms
(Additional beaten egg may be needed to bind the drier ingredients)

In a large mixing bowl, combine the fish or meat with the onion, oats and selection (if any) from the optional list. Beat the egg and stir into the mix. For a smooth-textured burger, whizz using a hand blender to make a thick, smooth paste.

To form the patties, flour the inside of a mug, drop in a dessertspoon of burger mix and sprinkle in a little more flour. Firmly squash down the mix using the blunt end of a rolling pin or back of a spoon. Run a rounded-end knife around the sides of the mix, invert the mug and a formed pattie will drop out. Repeat for the rest of the mix.

Heat a little olive oil in a non-stick frying pan. Place the burgers in the oil and cook for about 5 minutes on each side until golden brown.

Serve in a warmed pitta pocket or bread roll with salad or steamed vegetables. Delicious with Secret Agent Sauce (see page 147).

Tip If your child prefers the basic recipe smooth and you like the chunkier version, take out a couple of dessertspoons to whizz, then add your favourite combinations to the remaining mixture.

Fast food, not junk food

The thing is, 'junk' fast foods are often made from junk ingredients, but when you make your own at home, you know exactly what's in them. Take pizza, for example, which gets a bad press because the typical take-away is made with a base of refined white flour, bound with hydrogenated oils, lathered with cheap oily cheese, processed meats, barely fresh vegetables and often coated with salt. When you make it yourself, you can make a far healthier version.

Regular snacking

Toddlers needs to eat every 2–3 hours. Snacks are therefore a part of their dietary landscape. What you need to give them are snacks with a good GI (glycaemic index) rating (50 or below) to keep their little AA-sized batteries lasting longer. Choosing the wrong food to satisfy the munchies is a primary cause of childhood obesity so instead of instant-rush crisps, fizz and sweets, your child needs foods to help supply their brain with a steady stream of glucose and to prevent them from having temper tantrums that put Elton John to shame.

Keep 'good' snacks (e.g. boxes of raisins, carrot batons, apple slices or satsuma segments) to hand, with a selection tucked in your buggy sack or car glovebox, so you're not tempted to rush into a corner shop and buy one of the glinting fat/sugar/salt-laden packets on offer.

Pizza

A hit with all the family, there are limitless variations of what to put on a pizza – below are just a few suggestions. You can include the chosen topping in with the basic tomato sauce (and whizzing to a smoother paste) or sprinkle on top before adding the cheese so that they're easy to see.
Makes 3–4 servings (1 large or 4 individual pizzas)

FOR THE BASE
Double the quantities of
No-salt Breadsticks dough
(see page 126) and add:
25g (1oz) whole or chopped
sunflower seeds and
pumpkin seeds
or
Make up one 500g (18oz)
pack of granary bread mix
(this will be too much dough
for one portion – either
make a few extra bread rolls
or make another pizza with
more sauce)

1 dessertspoon olive oil to
grease a baking tray

FOR THE BASIC TOPPING SAUCE
1 dessertspoon olive oil
100g (3½oz) onions
1–2 garlic cloves
200g (7oz) fresh or tinned
tomatoes
1 teaspoon chopped capers or
olives (optional)
1 teaspoon fresh or ½
teaspoon dried mixed herbs
½ teaspoon vinegar or
Worcester sauce
Freshly ground black pepper

TO SPRINKLE ON TOP OR BLEND IN
WITH THE TOPPING SAUCE
SELECT FROM
50g (2oz) courgette
50g (2oz) mushrooms
50g (2oz) red or green pepper

TO FINISH
75g (3oz) hard cheese

Preheat the oven to 220°C/425°F/gas mark 7. Make the dough, adding the seeds before the water (if using a bread mix follow the packet instructions). Set aside to allow to rise.

To make the topping, heat the oil in a medium saucepan. Peel and chop the onions, crush the garlic and cook until soft. Chop the tomatoes and add with the capers or olives (if using), herbs, vinegar or Worcester sauce and black pepper. Stir well and bring to a simmer.

Chop your selected topping ingredients and if you want a smooth sauce, add to the tomato mix and whizz.

Flour a clean work surface and either stretch or roll out the dough to the size of your baking tray. Oil the baking tray and put the dough on to the tray, stretching to fit as needed.

Spread the sauce on the base, sprinkle with the topping if not blended in the sauce (encourage your child to do this to make it their handiwork) and grate the cheese on top.

Bake for 25–30 minutes until the dough edges sound hollow when you tap them and the cheese begins to brown.

Serve, or cool and freeze. Delicious hot or cold.

Fish Cakes

Unlike burgers, a good fish cake should be a meal in itself, with a nice balance of fish, potato and veg. You can vary this recipe by replacing the fish with a lean minced meat.
Makes 8 fish cakes

100g (3½oz) potato or sweet
potato
25g (1oz) carrot
25g (1oz) leek
25g (1oz) baby sweetcorn
25g (1oz) broccoli or peas

50g (2oz) skinless white fish
A little chopped dill (optional)
½ beaten egg
50g (2oz) breadcrumbs
1–2 teaspoons olive oil
A little plain flour

Wash, peel and chop the potato and carrot. Steam for 5 minutes.

Finely slice the leek, baby sweetcorn, broccoli (or peas), add to the potatoes and carrot and steam for a further 5 minutes.

Check the fish for bones and finely chop. Add to the steamer with the dill, if using, and cook for 5 more minutes.

Meanwhile, beat the egg. If making your own breadcrumbs, blitz 50g (2oz) bread in the chopping attachment of a hand blender and set aside.

Either mash or blend the vegetable and fish mix depending on how coarse or smooth your child prefers it, adding in the egg.

Heat the olive oil in a frying pan. Flour your hands then scoop a dessertspoon-size dollop of the mix and form a patty (the mixture will be quite moist) then drop into the bread-crumbs to coat. Fry on each side for 3–4 minutes until golden.

Meat Skewer Kebabs

Makes 3–4 skewers

100g (3½oz) beef, lamb or turkey

8 button mushrooms

Red, yellow or orange pepper

50g (2oz) broccoli florets or a few mangetout

1 courgette

50g (2oz) fresh or tinned (in natural juice) pineapple or fresh mango

1–2 tablespoons olive oil

Preheat the grill. Rinse and chop the meat, vegetables and fruit to roughly 2cm (¾in) cubes. Thread on to skewers ensuring you have a bright combination of colours.

Brush with olive oil and grill for 6–7 minutes on each side until the meat is golden brown and cooked through.

Serve in pitta breads with salad or with steamed vegetables.

Note Never give a young child a skewer – use a fork to slide the kebab off the skewer before serving.

Home-made Oven Chips

King Edwards, Maris Piper, Wilja and Pentland Dell are all great varieties for home-made oven chips. This method is part-boil, part-roast which lowers the saturated fat content and avoids using a vat of hot oil.

Makes 1–2 servings

1 large potato

1 tablespoon sunflower oil

Preheat the oven to 200°C/400°F/gas mark 6. Grease a non-stick baking tray with half the oil and heat in the oven. Bring a pan of water to the boil while you wash and peel the potato and cut into chunky chips. Part-cook the chips in water by simmering for 3 minutes. Drain and dry off with kitchen paper. Place the chips on the baking tray and drizzle with the remaining oil, ensuring they are coated. Bake for 15 minutes, until golden and crispy, turning once, halfway through. Transfer to a plate and allow to cool before serving.

Drinks

You may know 5 pieces of fruit a day is the aim, however your toddler may not be so wise. Drinks are a great way to sneak a mix of fruit into their diets. Here are 4 fruity drinks to tempt your little ones.

Apple and Mint Lassi

Lassi originates from India, so it's deliciously refreshing on a hot day with the added benefit of being packed with calcium and vitamin D. The basic idea is fruit and yogurt and works well with most fruit. Use organic live yogurt. If your child doesn't like or can't have dairy try a soya-based yogurt.
Makes 1 tall drink

½ dessert apple
2–3 sprigs of fresh mint
3 tablespoons natural yogurt

200ml (7fl oz) iced water (or water and ice)

Wash and core the apple (no need to peel). Combine all the ingredients in a liquidiser and blitz until smooth.
   Serve immediately with a sprig of mint to garnish.

Strawberry Smoothie

The base of the smoothie is banana with a selection of fruit and some juice to keep it liquid. Smoothies are best chilled and work as well with frozen fruit. The variations are endless but here's a simple one to get you started.
Makes 1 tall drink

1 medium banana
50g (2oz) strawberries (fresh or frozen)

200ml (7fl oz) apple juice

Combine all the ingredients in a liquidiser and blitz until smooth. If using fresh strawberries, include a few ice cubes to cool the drink.

Peach Melba Milk Shake

Milk shakes may sound old-fashioned in this brave new world of smoothies, but made with fresh fruit, they are fab.
Makes 1 tall drink

1 peach
4–5 raspberries (fresh or frozen)

200ml (7fl oz) cow's milk, goat's milk or soya milk

Peel and de-stone the peach. Combine all the ingredients in a liquidiser and blitz until smooth. Serve immediately.
   For a thick shake or a summer treat, replace 50ml (2fl oz) of milk with a scoop of real dairy ice-cream.

Tropical Sunshine

The base of these is fruit and I can't think of a combination that would not work – it's a great way to enjoy seasonal fruits as well as a tropical treat even in winter.
Makes 1 tall drink

50g (2oz) fresh mango
50g (2oz) fresh pineapple

200ml (7fl oz) grapefruit or orange juice

Combine all the ingredients in a liquidiser and blitz until smooth. Serve immediately
   Some children (and adults) find grapefruit juice too bitter so replace with orange juice, if preferred.

Snacks

Everybody from Scooby Doo to Homer Simpson likes a snack. Your little ones are no exception. With the amount of running around and growing taking place it's important to keep energy levels balanced by storing some treats and having some handy recipes for when they come roaring into the kitchen.

Cheesy Footballs

Makes about 30
(these will freeze or keep in an airtight tin for up to a week)

50g (2oz) butter or margarine, chilled
100g (3½oz) wholemeal plain flour
50g (2oz) cheddar cheese
Pinch of mustard (optional)
1 egg yolk (to use the egg white, see Tempura Vegetables on page 152)

TO MAKE COLOURED BALLS
1 teaspoon finely chopped or puréed red pepper or spinach
2–3 teaspoons milk if needed

Grate the butter into the flour and rub in until the mixture resembles breadcrumbs. Grate the cheese, stir into the flour and butter and add the mustard, if using. Add the egg yolk and draw the mixture together to form a dough. If you are making coloured balls, divide the dough and mix in the chopped or puréed pepper or spinach into half of the dough (adding the extra milk only if needed).

Put the dough in a plastic bag and chill for about 30 minutes. Meanwhile preheat the oven to 200°C/400°F/gas mark 6. Lightly grease several baking trays with a little olive oil or butter.

Lightly flour your hands, pull off a teaspoonful of dough and roll into a ball. Place on the baking tray and repeat using all the dough. Bake for 20 minutes until lightly golden. Transfer to a wire rack and allow to cool before serving.

Tip The dough can also be rolled out and shaped using a biscuit cutter to any shape and become a savoury version of Funny Face Biscuits on page 166.

Oat and Raisin Cookies

Makes 14 cookies
(these will freeze or keep in an airtight tin for up to a week)

50g (2oz) butter
100g (3½oz) caster sugar
1 egg, beaten
50g (2oz) self-raising flour
175g (6oz) porridge oats
125g (4½oz) raisins
½ teaspoon cinnamon

Preheat the oven to 180°C/350°F/gas mark 4. Lightly grease two non-stick baking trays.

In a large mixing bowl, cream together the butter and sugar until light and fluffy.

Add the beaten egg gradually and beat until well combined. Sift the flour into the creamed mixture, add the oats, raisins and cinnamon and mix well.

Place dessertspoonfuls of the mixture well apart on the prepared baking trays and flatten them slightly with the back of a spoon. Bake for 15 minutes.

Leave the cookies to cool slightly on the baking trays, before transferring to a wire rack. Leave to cool completely before serving.

Speedy Savoury Pancakes

Makes 1–2 servings

40ml (1½fl oz) whole milk
25g (1oz) wholemeal or white
  self-raising flour
1 small egg
25g (1oz) medium hard
  cheese

1 tablespoon finely chopped
  vegetables (choose from
  broccoli, sweetcorn,
  peppers, peas, tomato)
15g (¾oz) butter

In a small mixing bowl gradually add the milk to the flour to avoid lumps. Beat the egg and add half to the mixture.

Grate the cheese and stir through the mixture. Add the vegetables.

Heat the butter in a non-stick frying pan. Pour a dessertspoonful of the mixture into the pan; it should spread to about 5cm (2in). Repeat to form another 2–3 pancakes, leaving a little space between each. Cook until they start to set and bubbles begin to form (about 3 minutes) then turn and cook for a further 3 minutes until golden.

Mini Stuffed Mushrooms

Makes 6 stuffed mushrooms
(not suitable for freezing)

6 large button mushrooms
A little olive oil
1 dessertspoon fresh
  breadcrumbs

15g (¾oz) hard cheese,
  grated
1 garlic clove, crushed
1 teaspoon chopped chives

Wash and dry the mushrooms and remove the stalks. Brush the head with olive oil and gently grill until they begin to brown and soften a little (but not collapse).

Combine the breadcrumbs, cheese, garlic and chives in the chopping bowl of a hand blender and whizz. Use a teaspoon to pack the stuffing mixture into each mushroom and grill until golden.

Real Fruit Tarts

These can also be jam tarts (look out for some excellent low-sugar, high-in-real-fruit jams from specialist organic shops). Remember pastry should remain cold until it goes into a hot oven so make sure that the fat is chilled or if you have time make the dough in advance, pop it in a plastic bag and chill or even freeze until needed.

Makes about 20 tarts

FOR THE PASTRY
100g (3½oz) butter or
  margarine (very cold)
200g (7oz) wholemeal plain
  flour
4–6 tablespoon very cold
  water

2 bun baking trays
FOR THE FILLING
Approx 200ml (7fl oz) fruit
  purée simmered to drive off
  excess liquid, then cooled
Pinch of spice, e.g. cinnamon
  or ginger (optional)

Grate the butter or margarine into the flour and lightly rub in. Add the water a little at a time and use a round-ended knife or metal spoon to mix and form a dough ball. You will need to use your fingers towards the end. Wrap in a plastic bag and either chill for at least 30 minutes or freeze for use on another day.

Preheat the oven to 220°C/425°F/gas mark 7.

Roll out the pastry and cut into discs using an 8cm (3¼in) pastry cutter. Place in the bun trays. Put 1–2 teaspoons of fruit purée mixed with the spice or 1 frozen cube of fruit purée in each case. Bake for 15–20 minutes. Allow to cool on a wire rack.

Fun with food and party ideas

You've probably had a good old belly laugh at cookery books suggesting that parents present their children with complicated food sculptures. Ah – if only you had the time to fashion hair bows out of courgettes. In theory, though, it's a good idea because around this time your toddler's imagination begins to kick in – and one way to convince your child to eat is to tap into their fantasy world.

One of the problems with creating Picasso-like works of art is that you could find your child loves them so much they won't want to eat them. Some creations, like faces or clocks, are quick and easy to prepare (see Making mealtime a learning time on page 155); however, sometimes just re-naming the dishes makes them instantly more palatable. It's not spaghetti – it's shoelaces, slippery worms, or witch's hair. It's not just fish pie, it's Pingu's lunch or Bob the Builder's dinner.

Another way to get them to eat is by tapping into their fantasy world. It's not broccoli, it's a tree. A pea becomes a boulder. Mash becomes a mountain. Suddenly, dinner is not just a pile of vegetables – it's a giant's feast. Noises are another way to get them to eat their meals. After each mouthful, they can be a jeep and go 'beep, beep' or a sheep and go 'baa'. You can also get an array of decorated utensils to have fun with (like an aeroplane or digger spoon). These can also come to life in their fantasy world and you may just find them helpful with a food that is proving difficult.

While it's one way to get your child's eye connecting to their stomach, you don't want to make this a habit as mealtimes could turn to custard if every meal isn't some new, exciting adventure. Remind them that enjoying good-quality food is itself one of life's great pleasures.

Dragon's Blood Soup

I have happy childhood memories of fancy dress Halloween parties with a themed feast. Dragon's blood soup became a favourite not just on Halloween, but to warm up winter tea-time too. To our neighbour's relief Mum couldn't find a dragon so substituted tomatoes.

Makes 4–6 servings

400g (14oz) ripe tomatoes	500ml (18fl oz) milk or milk
1 medium onion (approx.	and stock (see page 118)
100g/3½oz)	½ teaspoon brown sugar
25g (1oz) butter, margarine or	1 small bay leaf
1 tablespoon olive oil	1 dessertspoon lemon juice
25g (1oz) cornflour	Freshly ground black pepper

Wash and finely chop the tomatoes and onion. Melt the butter or heat the oil and cook the tomatoes and onion until soft, then whizz with a hand blender.

Blend the cornflour with a little of the milk, ensuring there are no lumps then make up to 500ml (18fl oz) with the rest of the milk, stock if using, and sugar. Pour into the tomato purée, add the bay leaf and bring to the boil, stirring continuously. Simmer for 10 minutes, stirring occasionally. Towards the end of the 10 minutes, add the lemon juice and black pepper to taste. Remove the bay leaf.

Serve with Witch's Fingernails (see page 166). A sprinkling of grated cheese once served makes a special treat.

Other soup ideas

Dinosaur Swamp Soup
Use the Cheesy, Broccoli, Cauliflower and Potato recipe on page 38 without the added salt.

Wiggly Worm Soup
Make a chicken noodle soup with chicken stock, a little extra finely chopped cooked chicken, broken-up spaghetti and add some finely chopped vegetables such as broccoli or spring onion or a few peas or some sweetcorn.

Snail, Star and Daisy Sarnies

Sandwiches make a quick snack, light meal or handy feed-all, for family gatherings and birthday parties. Sure, there's the classic square or triangle cut, but here are a few more ideas to intrigue a young 'un.

Snails
Spread a slice of bread with a sticky filling such as jam, Marmite and butter, honey (only for children over 12 months) or hummus.

Cut off the crusts (see Witch's Fingernails on page 166 for an idea for what to do with them), then roll the bread up like a Swiss roll. Cut across with a sharp knife to reveal the spiral discs and serve on a plate of lettuce leaves.

Stars
Make sandwiches with your chosen fillings then use a star-shaped cookie cutter. Cut-out shapes work well with most other cookie cutters but remember to choose one that doesn't waste too much.

Daisies
You will need a large flower-shaped cutter and a small round cutter. Cut two bread slices using the flower cutter then cut out a central hole from just one slice. Spread the flower with a colourful filling (e.g. sliced cheese, ham, jam) then complete the sandwich with the other slice so you can see the filling at the centre of the daisy.

Filling ideas
Egg mayonnaise with cress (hardboiled egg, mashed with pasteurised mayo).
Grated cheese, grated carrot, diced ham, parsley.
Cream cheese, lemon zest, parsley and steamed salmon.
Tuna, mayo, sweetcorn, lettuce.

Witch's Fingernails

Sounds interesting? Good, because these couldn't be simpler and I have to credit my mum for the exciting name given to what are actually the discarded crusts from party sandwiches (see page 165)!

Crusts cut from slices of bread
15g (³/₄oz) butter

A little yeast extract (Marmite) or 1 teaspoon jam

Grill the crusts until golden and crunchy. Melt the butter and stir in the Marmite or jam until runny. Use a pastry brush to paint on the Marmite or jam 'nail varnish'. Serve on their own, as a purée dipper, or on the side of a main dish or soup. Older children will love painting the Witch's Fingernails themselves, so serve the 'varnish' in an egg cup.

Real Fruit Ice Pops

Some children go off fruit, maybe because it seems boring compared to all the other sweet things available. Commercial ice lollies are typically riddled with synthetic colours and flavours; organic fruit pops are virtually unheard of. To make your own, most recipes suggest adding caster or icing sugar. I've found they can lack flavour without sweetness, but I prefer to use apple juice instead of refined sugar.
Makes 8 mini pops (you can buy ice pop moulds from most department stores or from specialist kitchen supply shops – check the volume of liquid your set needs)

200ml (7fl oz) seasonal fruit purée (see stage 1)

400ml (14fl oz) apple juice

Combine the purée and apple juice in a liquidiser and blitz. Pour into the moulds and freeze until solid.

For super-quick ice pops, use frozen fruit purées or crush in a few cubes of ice, so the mixture is very cold even before they're put in the freezer.

Crispy Cakes

These will bring back memories – they're easy to make and great for a young child who wants to learn how to cook. Add a couple of mini choc eggs to turn into a bird's nest.
Makes 15 cakes

75g (3oz) butter
2–3 tablespoons golden syrup
200g (7oz) plain or milk chocolate

100g (3¹/₂oz) corn flakes or rice crispies
15 paper cup-cake cases

In a large saucepan, melt the butter, then reduce to a low heat. Add the syrup and the chocolate (broken into chunks) and stir until melted. Remove from the heat and stir in the cereal. Spoon into the paper cases and leave to cool.

Funny Face Biscuits

This simple recipe is a great way to get children involved in cooking.
Makes about 20

200g (7oz) self-raising flour
100g (3¹/₂oz) caster sugar
100g (3¹/₂oz) butter or margarine (chilled)

1 small egg
1 tablespoon lemon juice

Preheat the oven to 180°C/350°F/gas mark 4. Lightly grease a couple of baking trays.

Mix the flour and sugar and grate in the butter or margarine. Use your fingers to rub in until the mixture resembles breadcrumbs. Beat the egg and add, with the lemon juice, to the flour mixture and bring it together with your hands to form a firm dough.

Sprinkle the work surface with a little more flour and roll out. Use cookie cutters to shape, place on the baking trays and bake for 10–15 minutes until lightly golden. Leave to cool on a wire rack and store in an airtight tin.

Cup Cakes, Fairy Cakes and Butterfly Cakes

Makes 14–16

BASIC CUP CAKE RECIPE:
100g (3½oz) butter or margarine
100g (3½oz) caster sugar

2 medium eggs
100g (3½oz) self-raising flour
Paper cup-cake cases

Preheat the oven to 190°C/375°F/gas mark 5 and set out the paper cases into cup-cake trays.

Cream the butter and sugar until pale in colour and creamy in texture. Beat in the eggs one at a time then fold in the flour (sift first if there are any lumps). Half-fill each paper bun case and bake for about 20 minutes until firm (check they are cooked through by inserting a metal skewer into one of the buns – if it comes out clean they're ready). Allow to cool. If you plan to freeze them do so at this point, before decorating. For decorating ideas, see below and right.

Butterfly cakes

Decorates 14–16 cup cakes

14–16 cup cakes (see recipe left)
FOR BUTTERFLY CAKE DECORATION
25g (1oz) butter or margarine
50g (2oz) icing sugar

Choose flavours from:
2 chunks melted chocolate
1 teaspoon cocoa (adding a little milk if too dry)
2–3 drops vanilla extract
1 teaspoon orange or lemon juice

Cream the butter and icing sugar together – for speed combine in the chopping bowl of a hand blender and whizz. Alternatively beat with a fork until pale, smooth and creamy. Add the chosen flavouring.

To make the butterfly wings, cut a slice from the top of each cake and cut in half. Place a blob of icing in the centre of cake top and arrange the wings at angles on top.

Decorating fairy cakes

For speed you can get on with icing these yourself, for fun involve your child in baking and decorating. It'll be messy and their idea of stylish will probably resemble modern art.

Decorates 14–16 cup cakes

14–16 cup cakes (see recipe above)
TO DECORATE
2 tablespoons icing sugar
2–3 teaspoons water or fruit juice

Natural food colouring (optional), found in specialist organic shops and some supermarkets
Selection of colourful dried fruit, naturally coloured cake sprinkles or small chocolate shapes

Sift the icing sugar and gradually stir in the water or juice until smooth and runny enough to be drizzled from a teaspoon. Add the optional food colourings. If using dried fruits cut into sprinkle-sized pieces.

Drizzle the icing on to each cake and decorate.

Birthday Surprise Cake

This quick-to-make cake will delight children of all ages and adults too. Simply vary the surprises at the end of the streamers to suit the age of the guests.

Makes 16 child or 8 adult portions
(suitable for freezing before you decorate)

BASIC CAKE MIX
225g (8oz) caster sugar
225g (8oz) butter or
  margarine (check it is
  suitable for baking)
4 medium eggs
350g (12oz) self-raising flour
2 tablespoons milk (or orange
  juice if avoiding milk)
25g (1oz) butter or margarine
  to grease the cake ring

FOR THE CHOCOLATE MARBLE
1 rounded tablespoon cocoa

FOR THE PALE MARBLE
3–4 drops vanilla extract or
  grated rind (zest) of 1
  unwaxed lemon or orange

FOR THE SURPRISES
Small gift for each guest
  wrapped in coloured paper
  with a streamer attached

FOR THE ICING
225g (8oz) icing sugar
1 tablespoon warm water or
  orange juice (adding more
  as needed)

Preheat the oven to 180°C/350°F/gas mark 4. Use the extra butter or margarine to grease the inside of a non-stick 25cm (10in) cake ring.

Fast method

Measure the basic ingredients into the bowl of a food processor and beat with the plastic blade until smooth and creamy (2–3 minutes). Spoon out half into a mixing bowl and add the cocoa and beat for another minute (adding a little more milk if needed). Add the vanilla or citrus rind to the remaining mixture.

Traditional method

Combine the sugar and butter, beat with a fork until pale and creamy. Beat the eggs and slowly add. Sift the flour into the mixture, adding the milk as needed to make a smooth, stiff creamy mix. Scoop half into a separate mixing bowl and continue as above.

Using a dessertspoon, place spoonfuls of the each mixture alternately into the mould until all the mix has been used. Drag the spoon once through the cake mixture to create the marble effect (don't be tempted to stir further as you will end up with one colour rather than two!).

Bake for 30–35 minutes until well risen. To check it is cooked, insert a skewer into the mixture – it should come out clean.

Leave to cool a little then tap round the mould before turning out on a wire cooling rack.

Make the icing and use a wet palette knife to smooth over the cake.

Decorate as desired.

Directory

General advice on parenting

Babycentre
www.babycentre.co.uk

Mumsnet
www.mumsnet.com

Mother & Baby
www.motherand
babymagazine.com

NHS Direct
(For nurse advice)
Tel: 0845 4647
www.nhsdirect.co.uk

Guidance on Food Safety and Nutrition

Food Standards Agency
UK Headquarters
Aviation House
125 Kingsway
London WC2B 6NH
Switchboard:
020 7276 8000
Emergencies only:
020 7270 8960
General website:
www.food.gov.uk

Eatwell
(Offers advice and help to make healthier choices)
www.eatwell.gov.uk

Sure Start
(A government programme to deliver the best start in life for every child, bringing together early education, childcare, health and family support.)
www.surestart.gov.uk

Breast feeding advice

The National Childbirth Trust
Alexandra House
Oldham Terrace
Acton, London W3 6NH
Tel: 0870 7703236
Enquiry Line:
0870 444 8707
Membership line:
08709 908040
Breastfeeding Line:
0870 444 8708
www.nctpregnancy
andbabycare.com

Active Birth Centre
25 Bickerton Road
London N19 5JT
Tel: 020 7281 6760
www.activebirthcentre.com
mail@activebirthcentre.com

Midwivesonline.com
(For midwives, pregnancy and parenting and for products)
Jubilee Mill, North Street,
Bradford BD1 4EW
www.midwivesonline.com

La Leche League
(For parents in US and Canada)
1400 N. Meacham Road,
Schaumburg, IL 60173-4808
USA
Tel: (847) 519-7730
www.lalecheleague.org

Australian Breastfeeding Association
P.O. Box 4000
Glen Iris, Victoria 3146
Australia
Tel: (03) 9885 0855
From outside Australia
+61 3 98850855
www.breastfeeding.asn.au

Plunket
(For parents in New Zealand)
National Office
Level 5 Payroll House
126-132 Lambton Quay
PO Box 5474 Wellington
New Zealand
Tel: 64 04 471 - 0177
Fax: 64 04 471 - 0190
www.plunket.org.nz

Advice for vegetarian and vegan parents

The Vegetarian Society of the United Kingdom
Parkdale, Dunham Road
Altrincham, Cheshire
WA14 4QG
United Kingdom
Tel: 0161 925 2000
www.vegsoc.org

The Vegan Society
Donald Watson House
7 Battle Road
St Leonards-on-Sea
East Sussex TN37 7AA
www.vegansociety.com
Tel: 01424 427393

E numbers and additives

(Very handy website on which you can search additives by name or E number)
www.bryngollie.freeserve.
co.uk

Allergies and intolerances

The Hyperactive Children's Support Group
71 Whyke Lane
Chichester
West Sussex PO19 7PD
Tel: 01243 551313
www.hacsg.org.uk

Allergy UK
No 3 White Oak Square
London Road
Swanley, Kent
BR8 7AG
United Kingdom
www.allergyuk.org
Allergy Help line:
01322 619864
Chemical Sensitivity Help
line: 01322 619898

Anaphylaxis Society
The Anaphylaxis Campaign
PO Box 275
Farnborough
GU14 6SX
United Kingdom
Helpline: 01252 542029
www.anaphylaxis.org.uk

The British Allergy Foundation
Deepdene House
30 Bellegrove Road
Welling, Kent
DA16 3PY
Tel: 020 8303 8525
allergybaf@compuserve.com
www.allergyfoundation.com

The British Dietetic Association
5th Floor Charles House
148/9 Great Charles Street
Queensway
Birmingham
B3 3HT
(You can contact a Registered Dietitian via your local hospital or GP practice. For details of Registered Dietitians working in private practice in your area, please e-mail: info@bda.uk.com
www.bda.uk.com)

Independent Midwives Association
1 The Great Quarry,
Guildford
Surrey GUI 3XN
Tel: 01483 821104
information@
independentmidwives.org.uk

Food intolerance

www.foodintol.com

Dairy intolerance

The Allergy Site
www.theallergysite.co.uk

Gluten intolerance

Coeliac UK
PO Box 362
High Wycombe
Bucks HP11 2GW
Helpline: 0870 444 8804
www.coeliac.co.uk

When to wean

The Department of Health
Richmond House
79 Whitehall
London SW1A 2NL
Tel: 020 7210 4850
www.dh.gov.uk
dhmail@dh.gsi.gov.uk

The U.S. Department of Health and Human Services
200 Independence Avenue, S.W.
Washington, D.C. 20201
Tel: 202-619-0257
Toll Free: 1-877-696-6775
www.os.dhhs.gov

ACT Health (Australia)
ACT Health
GPO Box 825
Canberra City ACT 2601
+61 2 6207 5111
www.health.act.gov.au

World Health Organisation
The United Nations
(Specialised agency for health)
www.who.int/en

Research into weaning and food preference development

University Of Birmingham
Dr Gillian Harris
Department of Applied
Developmental Psychology
The University of
Birmingham
Edgbaston, Birmingham
B15 2TT
0121 414 3344

Monell Chemical Senses Institute
Monell Chemical Senses
Center
3500 Market Street
Philadelphia,
PA 19104-3308
USA
www.monell.org
Tel: +001 (215) 898-6666

For more information on organic food

The Organic Food Federation
31 Turbine Way, EcoTech
Business Park
Swaffham, Norfolk
PE37 7XD
Tel: 01760 720444
www.orgfoodfed.com

Soil Association
Bristol House
40-56 Victoria Street
Bristol BS1 6BY
Tel: 0117 314 5000
info@soilassociation.org
www.soilassociation.org

Organic Farmers & Growers
Elim Centre
Lancaster Road
Shrewsbury, Shropshire
SY1 3LE
Tel: 0845 330 5122 (local rate call)
www.organicfarmers.org.uk

Demeter
Demeter Scheme
Coordinator
17 Inverleith Place
EDINBURGH
EH3 5QE
Tel /fax: 0131 6243921
www.biodynamic.
org.uk/Demeter.htm

Fresh Daisy
Kinetic House
Theobald Street
Elstree, Herts
WD6 4PJ
Tel: 0870 240 7028
www.daisyfoods.com

Eostre Organics (Farming Co-operative)
Unit 2
North Side Hangars
Old Buckenham Airfield
Abbey Rd
Old Buckenham
nr Attleborough
Norfolk
NR17 1PU
Tel: 01953 456294
www.eostreorganics.co.uk

The Baby Friendly Initiative
(This is a global programme
of UNICEF and the World
Health Organisation which
works with the health
services to improve practice
so that parents are enabled
and supported to make
informed choices about
how they feed and care
for their babies. In the UK,
the Baby Friendly Initiative
is commissioned by various
parts of the health service
to provide advice, support,
training, networking,
assessment and
accreditation.)
www.babyfriendly.org.uk

First Aid for Infants

The Red Cross
(The British Red Cross is a
recognised market leader
in health and safety, and
the world's largest first aid
training provider.)
www.redcrossfirstaid
training.co.uk

A guide to making your
own infant first aid kit
www.babycentre.co.uk

Teething advice

www.askbaby.com

Advice on buying baby
teething products
www.teething-babies.co.uk

Index

Acknowledgements

Big thanks for all the mums, dads and babies who inspired this book, for all your questions and shared weaning experiences – the good, bad and ugly!

Sincere thanks to Ali Hanan, writer, journalist and mum of Luka, Rosa and big kid Dizzy.

Bruce, thanks for the hard work on the book, dedication to Fresh Daisy and endless support – you make me laugh. Sorry the hip-hop styley reference was cut.

To Alison Fenton, Sandra Lane, Lizzie Harris, Jacqueline Bellefontaine and Krissy Schmidt – thanks for all your hard work.

Big shout to the mighty Vickster, Mark, Jo, Seb, Quent, Sabine and Peter. Cheers to all at Create, especially head honcho Boyd – maybe VCs aren't so bad.

To Guy – for your vision and positive approach.

To all at Kyle Cathie – especially Muna, for the personable whip cracking and Homer impersonations.

To Green Baby (0870 240 6894/www.greenbaby.co.uk) for the loan of the baby clothes
and
Ezee-Reach Ltd (01908 565001/www.ezee-reach.com) for the springy cutlery on p111–112.

Sincere thanks for the expert guidance from Dr Anita Macdonald, Head of Research Dietetics, Birmingham Children's Hospital.

Finally thanks to supermodels Ben, Zen, Rosa, Rosa, Lily, Amy, Jack, Josh, Harry and Alice – something for your parents to tease you about when you're 18.